RAID ON THE ARTICULATE

RAID ON THE

> And so each venture
> Is a new beginning, a raid on the inarticulate.
> T. S. Eliot, *East Coker*

ARTICULATE

Comic Eschatology in Jesus and Borges

John Dominic Crossan

WIPF & STOCK · Eugene, Oregon

ACKNOWLEDGMENTS

Grateful acknowledgment is made to the following for permission to reprint selections included in this book:

E. P. DUTTON & COMPANY, INC. for 2 lines from "Heraclitus"; 3 lines from "Cambridge"; 6 lines from "To Israel"; 4 lines from "Israel"; 2 lines from "Plain Things" in *In Praise of Darkness* by Jorge Luis Borges. Translated by Norman Thomas di Giovanni. Copyright © 1969, 1970, 1971, 1972, 1973, 1974 by Emecé Editores S. A. & Norman Thomas di Giovanni. Reprinted by permission of E. P. Dutton & Co., Inc.

HARCOURT BRACE JOVANOVICH, INC. for permission to reprint 2 lines from "East Coker" in *Four Quartets* by T. S. Eliot. Copyright 1943 by T. S. Eliot. Renewed 1971 by Esme Valerie Eliot. Reprinted by permission of Harcourt Brace Jovanovich, Inc.

HARVARD UNIVERSITY PRESS for lines in both #501 and #883 from *The Poems of Emily Dickinson*, edited by Thomas H. Johnson, Cambridge, Mass.: The Belknap Press of Harvard University Press, © 1951, 1955 by the President and Fellows of Harvard College. Reprinted by permission of the publishers and the Trustees of Amherst College.

Wipf and Stock Publishers
199 W 8th Ave, Suite 3
Eugene, OR 97401

Raid on the Articulate
Comic Eschatology in Jesus and Borges
By Crossan, John Dominic
Copyright©1976 by Crossan, John Dominic
ISBN 13: 978-1-55635-822-7
Publication date 1/21/2008
Previously published by Harper & Row, 1976

HOLT, RINEHART AND WINSTON, INC. for 5 lines from "West-Running Brook" and 8 lines from "A Steeple on a House" from *The Poetry of Robert Frost*, edited by Edward Connery Lathem. Copyright 1928, 1947, © 1969 by Holt, Rinehart and Winston. Copyright © 1956 by Robert Frost. Copyright © 1975 by Lesley Frost Ballantine. Reprinted by permission of Holt, Rinehart and Winston, Publishers.

HOUGHTON MIFFLIN COMPANY for #1545 (2 lines) from "The Bible is an Antique Volume" from *Life and Letters of Emily Dickinson* by Martha Dickinson Bianchi. Copyright 1924 by Martha Dickinson Bianchi. Renewed 1952 Alfred Leete Lampson. Reprinted by permission of Houghton Mifflin Company.

LITTLE BROWN AND COMPANY for #1095 (2 lines) from *The Complete Poems of Emily Dickinson*, edited by Thomas H. Johnson. Copyright 1935 by Martha Dickinson Bianchi. Copyright © 1963 by Mary L. Hampson. Reprinted by permission of Little, Brown and Company.

MACMILLAN PUBLISHING COMPANY, INC. for 9 lines from "The Tower" in *Collected Poems* by William Butler Yeats. Copyright 1928 by Macmillan Publishing Co., Inc. Renewed 1956 by Georgie Yeats. Also for 8 lines from "Supernatural Songs." *Ibid.* Copyright 1934 by Bertha Georgie Yeats. Reprinted with permission of Macmillan Publishing Co., Inc.

NATIONAL COUNCIL OF THE CHURCHES OF CHRIST for quotations from the *Revised Standard Version of the Bible*. Copyright 1946, 1952, © 1971, © 1973.

NEW DIRECTIONS PUBLISHING CORPORATION for 10 lines from "Canto CXVI" in *The Cantos* by Ezra Pound. Copyright © 1966, © 1972, by Ezra Pound. Also for 9 lines from "The Words of the Lord to John on Patmos" in *Poems 1906–1926* by Rainer Maria Rilke, translated by J. B. Leishman. All Rights Reserved. Also for 3 lines from "Sonnets to Orpheus" in *Selected Works:II* by Rainer Maria Rilke, translated by J. B. Leishman. Copyright © 1960 by The Hogarth Press Ltd. All works reprinted by permission of New Directions Publishing Corporation.

ATHENEUM PUBLISHERS AND RICHARD HOWARD for 8 lines from "Prose for Borges" by Richard Howard in *TriQuarterly* 25 (Fall 1972). Originally from *Findings: A Book of Poems* by Richard Howard. Atheneum Publishers, 1971.

Permission to reprint is also gratefully acknowledged for parts of pp. 64–69 which originally appeared as "Jesus and Pacifism" in *No Famine in the Land*. Studies in honor of John L. McKenzie. Eds. J. W. Flanagan & A. Weisbrod Robinson. Missoula, Montana: Scholar Press, 1975. Copyright © 1975 by The Institute for Antiquity and Christianity, Claremont, California; and for parts of pp. 93–131 which originally appeared as "Parable, Allegory, and Paradox" in *Semiology and Parables*. Papers of the Vanderbilt University Conference, May 15–17, 1975. Ed. Daniel Patte. Pittsburgh, PA.: The Pickwick Press, 1976.

GROVE PRESS, INC for 6 lines from "Chess" in *A Personal Anthology* by Jorge Luis Borges. Copyright © 1967 by Grove Press, Inc. Reprinted by permission of Grove Press, Inc.

In memory
of my father
Daniel Joseph Crossan
1904–1971

It was he who revealed the power of poetry to me—the fact that words are not only a means of communication but also magic symbols and music.

Jorge Luis Borges, speaking of his father in *An Autobiographical Essay*

Contents

Preface	xiii
Theme	1
Variations	7

First Variation: Comedy and Transcendence   9
  Prelude: The People of the Secret   9

1. Tragedy
   A Greek Prejudice. Oedipus the King. The Dark Laughter of Zeus. The Victory of the Comic.   11

2. Comedy
   A Narrow Escape into Faith. The New Sense of the Comic. Dark Comedy. The Bias of Comedy. Death unto Resurrection.   16

3. Play
   The Search of Averroes. Homo Ludens. Homo Ludens Revisited. The Play of World. Breaks, Fissures, and Cracks. The Range of Comic Play.   23

4. Structure
   A System of Transformations. Structured Play. In the Beginning. The Ritual Process.   33

5. Literature
   Language as Play. Language as Supreme Play. The Conscience of Language. Defamiliarization. The New in Literature.   38

6. Transcendence
   A Great and Secret Plan. The Comic and the Holy. Biblical Laughter. At the Limits of Language.   43

  Postlude: The Secret of the People   50

Second Variation: Form and Parody   55

1. Iconoclasm

       No Graven Images. From Images to Words.
       No Graven Words.   55

2. Genre
   Literature as System. Generic Transformations.   60

3. Law
   Case Law. Case Interpretation. Case Parody.
   Beyond Morality.   63

4. Proverb
   Proverbial Wisdom? Paradoxical Aphorism.
   Beyond Wisdom.   69

5. Beatitude
   Proverb to Prayer. Blessed the Poor. From an
   Apocryphal Gospel.   73

6. Novel
   Footnotes in Stories. Reviews of Unwritten Books.
   Projects for Unwritten Books. Real and Imaginary
   Authors. Small, Hard, and Bright.   77

7. Mimesis
   The Book as Too Much. The Book as Too Little.
   The Mimetic Fallacy. Towards the Source.   89

Third Variation: Paradox and Parable   93

1. Paradox
   Contemporary Parable. Biblical Parable. Myth and
   Parable.   93

2. Parable
   Borges on Jesus. The Good Samaritan. Metonymy and
   Metaphor. Borges as Parabler.   99

3. Allegory
   Ideas or Images. Borges on Allegory. Motives for
   Allegory. Allegory as Play. Parables and Allegories.   115

Fourth Variation: Time and Finitude   133

1. Time
   Six Distinctions. Star-Time and Story-Time.   133

2. Circle
   Borges on Time. Circular Time. The Circle of Play. — 138

3. Line
   Prophecy and Apocalyptic. Immortality as Idolatry. Jesus on Apocalyptic. Borges on Immortality. — 144

4. Plot
   The Hidden Treasure. Other Stories, Other Treasures. Time and Theme. — 153

Fifth Variation: Person and Persona — 165

1. Persona
   Intention and Personality. Revelation's Imminence. — 165

2. Borges
   Borges and "Borges." Borges as "Borges." Borges and Comic Eschatology. — 170

3. Jesus
   Jesus, Christ, and Lord. The Historical Jesus. Jesus and Comic Eschatology. — 174

4. Orpheus
   Lyre and Voice. Play and Death. — 179

Notes — 183

Abbreviations, Editions, Bibliographies — 199

Index of Citations — 201

Index of Authors — 205

Preface

> Would you call this age a good one for unicorns?
> Peter S. Beagle, *The Last Unicorn*

For the last hundred years biblical criticism has meant historical criticism. The Bible was read self-consciously and self-critically against the historical background of its own time and its own progress. The fascinating successes of this method made it inevitable that it be considered not only as one very important methodology but rather as the only valid one for biblical studies.

The term literary criticism was, of course, always used in biblical exegesis, but mostly as a minor aid for historical reconstruction, and its results would hardly have been applauded as literary by scholars trained in comparative literature. Literary criticism in the full sense of the term sat with Cinderella in the biblical ashes.

Recent work in this country has begun to challenge this methodological monopoly, and the work of scholars such as Amos Wilder, Robert Funk, and Dan Via comes immediately and principally to mind. Indeed literary criticism not only urges historical criticism to give it equal room as partner in research; it also theorizes a little truculently about the primacy of language over history. Literature reminds history that it is language and text that binds the historical student with the historical subject and that it may be terribly naive to ignore that medium in which we all live, move, and have our being.

It is especially, but not exclusively, in structuralist literary criticism that this challenge to history's position as a supreme model for research has been expressed most forcibly. What if one took language instead of history as the master paradigm for critical activity? Frederic Jameson reacted to this proposal in *The Prison-House of Language* with this. "Language as a model! To rethink everything through once again in terms of linguistics! What is surprising, it would seem, is only that no one ever thought of doing so before; for of all the elements of consciousness and of social life, language would appear to enjoy some incomparable ontological priority, of a type yet to be determined." And if we are actually dealing with a shift in the master paradigms of our research we are in the midst of what Thomas S. Kuhn has described so well in his book *The Structure of Scientific Revolutions:* "a reconstruction that changes some of the field's most elementary theoretical generalizations as well as many of its paradigm methods and applications."

One might at this point suggest a major difference between German and American scholarship in their respective attitudes towards the older and more established historical biblical criticism. Admittedly, literary criticism, here as there, finds itself in a somewhat Oedipal situation. In Germany, however, the structuralist critics represented by Erhardt Güttgemanns and the "Generative Poetics" group at the University of Bonn look at historical criticism and think of it as their Laius. Most biblical scholars of a linguistic and literary persuasion in America think of it as their Jocasta. This explains no doubt a certain divergence in their respective angles of attack.

This book situates itself within this challenge posed by structuralist literary criticism to the monolithic ascendancy of historical criticism in biblical studies. And I admit that at the moment I am much more interested in structuralist philosophy than in structuralist methodology. The theory fascinates me although the practice often bores me. The book also indicates how theological syntheses might be developed just as well, or maybe much better, on the basis of structure as once they were on the foundations of history. The French philosopher Paul

Ricoeur has quoted with approval the statement of the structuralist critic A. J. Greimas that "there is perhaps a mystery *of* language, and this is a question for philosophy, there is no mystery *in* language." My present book is dedicated to that slender *perhaps*.

It also presumes, acknowledges, and appreciates the results of historical investigation into the teachings of Jesus. It will never use texts except those supported as authentic by the vast majority of the most critical historical scholarship. But the book claims that such texts are best understood not only within their own contemporary situation by comparative historical criticism but also, and indeed especially, in confrontation with texts within our own world which are functionally, generically, and philosophically on the same literary trajectory, that is, through comparative literary criticism. I am not making genetic and causal comparisons within the contacts of history but I am proposing systemic and generic relationships within the possibilities of language.

This work, then, continues and specifies the exploration of two preceding books, *In Parables* and *The Dark Interval*. The former book, the articles on which it was based, and some others mentioned in the terminal Notes for this present work give much greater details on the textual and hermeneutical problems involved in establishing the text for Jesus' parables. I have no intention of repeating those arguments here. The reader wishing fuller documentation for this book's interpretation of Jesus' stories is invited to those places but the invitation will not be constantly repeated.

A word on Notes. I have presented them with a view to the different needs of individual readers. There are no numbered footnotes in the text itself. This means that those who wish to read and run can do so without being accosted by tiny numbers pointing elsewhere. But the reader who needs references will find complete notes at the back of the book page by page. And a special word on the Indices. Borges's stories have often appeared in several of his anthologies. I cite his stories in the text by title alone but a glance at the index will give all the collections where a given story has appeared. I always quote from the first such collection indicated. So also with Jesus' parables. They are cited only by title and the varied versions are noted in the index. All of which is intended to keep the text as free from numbers as possible.

THEME

Franz Kafka

What is laid upon us is to accomplish the negative, the positive is already given.

Roland Barthes

What I claim is to live to the full the contradiction of my time, which may well make sarcasm the condition of truth.

No semiology which cannot, in the last analysis, be acknowledged as semioclasm.

The writer is not defined by the use of specialized tools which parade literature . . . but by the power of surprising, by some formal device, a particular collusion of man and nature, i.e., a meaning: and in this "surprise," it is form which guides, form which keeps watch, which instructs, which knows, which thinks, which "commits"; this is why form has no other judge than what it reveals.

George Poulet

I am above all attracted by those for whom literature is—by definition—a spiritual activity which must be gone beyond in its own depths, or, which, in failing to be gone beyond, in being condemned to the awareness of a non-transcendence, affirms itself as the experience and verification of a fundamental defeat.

John Barth

An artist may paradoxically turn the felt ultimacies of our time into material and means for his work—*paradoxically* because by doing so he transcends what has appeared to be his refutation, in the same way that the mystic who transcends finitude is said to be enabled to live, spiritually and physically, in the finite world.

E. M. Cioran

Venturing to the roots of the Vague, the novelist becomes an archeologist of absence, exploring the strata of what does not and cannot exist, unearthing the imperceptible, revealing it to our accessory and disconcerted eyes. An unconscious mystic? No such thing; for the mystic, if he describes his inner torments, focuses his expectation on an object within which he manages to anchor himself. . . . Abjuring his failures, converting his waking nights into a Way, not a hypostasis, he enters a region where he no longer has the sensation (the most painful of all) that *being* is forbidden him, that a pact between it and himself will never be possible. The novelist, on the contrary, knows only the periphery, the boundaries of being: that is why he is a writer. At his best moments, he explores the no man's land that stretches between these frontiers and those of literature.

Susan Sontag

The newer myth, derived from a post-psychological consciousness, installs within the activity of art many of the paradoxes involved in attaining an absolute state of being described by the great religious mystics. As the activity of the mystic must end in a *via negativa*, a theology of God's absence, a craving for the cloud of unknowing beyond knowledge and for the silence beyond speech, so art must tend toward anti-art, the elimination of the "subject" (the "object," the "image"), substitution of chance for intention, and the pursuit of silence.

Jerzy Peterkiewicz

Today the poet has more than ever to exercise the two faculties at his disposal: intuition and imagination. Both bring him close to the frontier of words and he learns from the first experience of silence that the real present cannot be entered unless it is reached through silence. The crisis, the sacrifice, and the *noche oscura* occur in the same vertical relationship with that other silence, at which the poet hurls his questions, supplications, and abuse. He is never answered, although like Job he believes in the Voice on the inscrutable side of silence.

5 Theme

A. R. AMMONS

I would suggest you teach that poetry leads us to the unstructured sources of our beings, to the unknown, and returns us to our rational, structured selves refreshed. Having once experienced the mystery, plenitude, contradiction, and composure of a work of art, we afterwards have a built-in resistance to the slogans and propaganda of over-simplification that have often contributed to the destruction of human life. Poetry is a verbal means to a non-verbal source. It is a motion to no-motion, to the still point of contemplation and deep realization. Its knowledges are all negative and, therefore, more positive than any knowledge. Nothing that can be said about it in words is worth saying.

VARIATIONS

First Variation:
Comedy and Transcendence

> Obviously there is no classification of the universe that is not arbitrary and conjectural. . . . We must go even further; we must suspect that there is no universe in the organic, unifying sense inherent in that ambitious word. If there is, we must conjecture its purpose; we must conjecture the words, the definitions, the etymologies, the synonymies of God's secret dictionary. But the impossibility of penetrating the divine scheme of the universe cannot dissuade us from outlining human schemes, even though we are aware that they are provisional.
>
> Jorge Luis Borges

At the start of *The Joyful Wisdom* Friedrich Nietzsche wrote that "there is perhaps still a future even for laughter." This section is based on that hope but in the somber awareness that today, about a hundred years later, there is perhaps still a future for very little else.

And I also presume that, since there is tragedy too great for tears, there must also be comedy too deep for laughter.

This double awareness is continuously present throughout the First Variation which intends to establish the theoretical background against which I plan to compare the two great parablers Jesus and Borges.

Prelude: The People of the Secret

When his 1944 volume of short stories or *Ficciones* went into its second edition in 1956 Borges added three new stories including one entitled "The Sect of the Phoenix." The most ancient sources, the story tells us, do not refer to the sect with this name but "speak only of the People of Custom or the People of the Secret." Indeed, the Phoenix epithet neither originated as far back in time nor diffused as widely in space as did this other title of "the Secret." Scholarly debates have confused the problem of the sect's identity. "Miklošić, in an overly famous page, has compared the[m] . . . with the gypsies. . . . [Or there is] the vulgar error (absurdly defended by Urmann) which sees in the Phoenix a derivative of Israel." But in any case the sectarians have integrated themselves into every nation in both East and West.

This ubiquitous sect shares no common color, has no common language, and reveres no common scripture. "Only this thing—the Secret—unites them and will unite them until the end of time." They do have both a myth and a ritual for their Secret. The myth, unfortunately, is a little vague and indefinite by now but it recalls something ("a punishment, or a pact, or a privilege, for the versions differ") about a God who will give eternity to those who faithfully observe a certain rite throughout their generations. And here we are at the very heart of the sect's destiny for: "The rite itself constitutes the Secret." Knowledge of this ritual Secret is not passed on pedagogically in the usual and expected ways for such solemn liturgical mysteries. Neither parents nor priests but "individuals of the lowest order" serve to initiate others into the Secret. Slaves, lepers, beggars, even children are the chosen teachers, and ruins, cellars, and doorways replace temples as propitious places for the rite's celebration. And this underlines the strangest aspect of the entire affair. "The Secret is sacred, but it is also somewhat ridiculous." The initiates celebrate the rite in furtive and clandestine ways and while there "are no respectable words to describe it, it is understood that all words refer to it, or better, that they inevitably allude to it." Just as the devotees of the Secret infiltrate all the people of the earth so the ritual of the Secret pervades all the languages of the world. There are, however, believers afraid to fulfill the ritual and there are others who despise themselves since they experience no such reluctance. "On the other hand, those sectarians who deliberately renounce the Custom and manage to engage in direct communication with the divinity enjoy a large measure of credit." When one considers the vast possibilities of time and space it is extraordinary that the Secret has not been lost somewhere during its long history. But, as the story concludes, "One commentator has not hesitated to assert that it is already instinctive."

What is this Secret, this Custom, and who are these sectarians of the Phoenix hidden among all the nations of the world?

1. TRAGEDY

I must acknowledge at once the ancient and venerable prejudice that exalts tragedy above comedy and gives the former a high seriousness long denied the latter. Consider, for example, the apodictic claim of Enid Welsford that, "the facts of life are tragic, and the human heart is proof against the comic spirit." But, having placed this assertion at the start of her social and literary history of *The Fool*, she can conclude about three hundred pages later that, "the serious hero focuses events, forces issues, and causes catastrophes; but the Fool by his mere presence dissolves events, evades issues, and throws doubt on the finality of fact." One wonders that an author writing in the mid-thirties of this century had no suspicion that the world needed a few less heroes and a few more fools.

In a recent essay Robert Martin, much more sensitive to the imperialism sedimented deep into language itself, notes that, "one speaks of poetry as distinct from comic poetry, of the novel contrasted to the comic novel. (Whoever spoke of The Tragic Novel?)" No such adjective is needed because it is assumed beyond contention that The Novel is serious, earnest, relevant, and sublimely tragic.

Hence this summary judgment from the English poet essayist Joseph Addison: "A perfect tragedy is the noblest production of human nature."

A Greek Prejudice

As is well known Plato wanted no dramatists in his ideal republic. All that appears here on earth is but a copy of the eternal forms which transcend our present experiences. But what if poets were allowed to portray on page or stage their fictional creations? Would there not be copies of copies and might not reality dissolve into a game of shifting mirrors leaving us wrapped in vertiginous relativity? But while Book 10 of *The Republic* attacks both tragedy and comedy from this basis it is clear that Plato considers tragedy the greater threat. Since it is obviously the more serious activity it must receive the greater and primary ("tragedians and the rest of the imitative tribe") castigation.

Aristotle, on the other hand, has no such inhibitions against the dramatists because of their imitation which, according to the *Poetics*, "is natural to man from childhood, one of his advantages over the lower animals being this, that he is the most imitative creature in the world, and learns at first by imitation. And it is also natural for all to delight in works of imitation." Such imitations are of human actions and, "This difference it is that distinguishes Tragedy and Comedy also; the one would make its personages worse, and the other better, than the men of the present day." How does Comedy imitate men worse than the average? "Worse, however, not as regards any and every sort of fault, but only as regards one particular kind, the Ridiculous, which is a species of the Ugly. The Ridiculous may be defined as a mistake or deformity not productive of pain or harm to others." But the prejudice for tragedy's ascendancy is quite clear. "Poetry . . . broke up into two kinds [Tragedy and Comedy] according to the differences of character in the individual poets; for the graver among them would represent noble actions, and those of noble personages; and the meaner sort the actions of the ignoble."

Think, then, of two justly famous examples of Greek tragedy and see if the tragic sense of life is a more important and adequate vision of our human condition than is any comic alternative.

Oedipus the King

Alister Cameron has offered this summary of Sophocles' magnificent play *Oedipus Tyrranus*. "He shows us a man who must find out who he is but who, by forces external and internal, is condemned to go through untold agony in the process of this finding, and then, having found out who he is, is forced to recognize that the agony is, in some mysterious part, of his own making. Historically, the play is a moment, a brilliant, terrible moment, in the long story of man's discovery of himself." If we are to believe in the iron absolute of tragic inevitability there must be no way out. It is because of this total closure of retreat that the play is so perfect. At the very start, Oedipus, king of Thebes, swears to save his city by finding and punishing the murderer of its previous king: himself. And there is the perfect tragic plot, the absolute trap. Either way lies agony. Not to find the murderer is tragic failure. To find the murderer is tragic success. But why is all this tragedy and not some terrible joke?

In Dublin's Abbey Theatre last summer I saw W. B. Yeats's translation of this play which was on its way to the Edinburgh Festival. Allowance had to be made for a lead actor who tended to out-herod Herod on the principle of when in doubt, shout. And more allowance had to be made for a certain cultural inability to accept guilt without responsibility and responsibility without knowledge. But, even granting all that, it was extremely difficult to discuss the play afterwards without a certain degree of elegant scurrility reappearing in the conversation. The awful tragedy of the hero who murdered his father and married his mother stands perilously close to an awfully bad joke.

Later that same summer I was reading a book by Eric S. Rabkin on *Narrative Suspense* which compounded the problem and at exactly the same point. His book intended to work out an integrated schema of generic possibilities based on the types of suspense implied structurally by each proposed genre. He placed tragedy and joke in the same generic category drawing attention to the discharge in the joke's punch line and the recognition scene in tragedy. "There are," he claimed, "very great differences between a joke and a tragedy, but the differences are in attitude, emphasis, and so forth, rather than in structure." The only distinction he himself suggests between them is that "when a work . . . concerns only the individual, the discharge releases laughter; when it reflects on all of society, the discharge releases 'fear and pity.' Aristotle made sure to include in his definition of tragedy the prescription that the protagonist be of high estate." His example is, once again, Oedipus. In Sophocles he is a king and society's fate hinges on his actions. Therefore, tragedy. But in an irreverent recording, "Tom Lehrer has deflated Oedipus by emphasizing him as an individual. By treating him in a light song, Lehrer identifies Oedipus, the emblem of society, with a figure of fun."

I find the argument that tragic plot and joke are generically close, at least with regard to structural suspense, very interesting but I do not find the individual (comic) and societal (tragic) distinction too persuasive. We all know that the death of a beloved individual can be tragic even when it is a totally private relationship. And, on the other hand, if it is not possible to laugh at the whole human race I do not know why so many people are reading Kurt Vonnegut. Indeed, Aristotle himself may have pointed to a more important distinction when he said that the comic should not be painful. Tragedy is a joke that hurts too much for laughter. And if drama demands a willing suspension of disbelief, then tragedy demands a willing or unwilling suspension of comedy. Henri Bergson claimed that "the comic demands something like a momentary anesthesia of the heart" in which intellect divorces itself from feeling and thereby finds most of the world ridiculous. But it is just as likely that the opposite is true. Tragedy demands and even creates a momentary anesthesia of the smile.

The Dark Laughter of Zeus

There is an obvious objection to all this. It is unfair to question the supposed supremacy of tragedy by noting how easily *Oedipus* can become an awful joke. Here, one might object, Freud has ruined Sophocles. Take, then, one more example but let us keep it, so to speak, in the family.

Antigone is the daughter of Oedipus and his mother Jocasta. She insists on burying her slain brother whom Creon, successor to Oedipus, has condemned to lie dishonored and unburied, the fate of a traitor. It is a clash, we say, of personal conscience against city law, it is the fidelity of right against the vindictiveness of might. Looking back over the horrors of this century one sympathizes fully with Antigone and judges her completely, if tragically, in the right. The play, we say, is the serene attestation of individual conscience over and against official policy.

But it is not at all clear that Sophocles saw matters as a clash between Antigone and Creon with prevailing right on one side over the other. Jean-Pierre Vernant interprets the play in a far more disturbing manner. "Neither the *nomoi* of Creon nor the *nomoi* of Antigone are sufficient. They are both but aspects of the *nomos* of Zeus. I would point out right away, to indicate my disagreement with the Hegelian position, that the *nomos* of Zeus cannot be meditation because it is absolutely incomprehensible and impenetrable from the human viewpoint." The play is not just Antigone against Creon but both against Zeus. It is not conscience against law but the awful truth that neither has any absolute status before the *nomos* or law of Zeus and neither has any right to invoke this incomprehensible law as its own unique corroboration. Once again the question returns. Is this tragedy or is it the dark and terrible laughter of Zeus? Is it the tragedy of mortals or the comedy of gods?

The Victory of the Comic

One can always hold theoretically the greater dignity and importance of tragedy but practically the comic will often prevail in any case. Two examples.

Many scholars maintain that Aristotle wrote a treatise on Comedy to match his study on Tragedy. This latter presently fills the *Poetics* but, they suggest, it was once its Book 1 with the diptych on Comedy as Book 2. Be that as it may, either Aristotle wrote such a work and it is now lost or we do not know for sure if he did or not. Which is mildly funny and a small but entirely appropriate victory for the lost or unwritten work on Comedy. A larger and even more appropriate one would have been its survival and the loss of the treatise on Tragedy.

16   Raid on the Articulate

At the end of Plato's *Symposium* the banquet almost breaks up in drunken disorder as "a great crowd of revellers arrived at the door, which they found just opened for some one who was going out. They marched straight into the party and seated themselves: the whole place was in an uproar and, losing all order, they were forced to drink a vast amount of wine." The narrator of the story is Aristodemus who, having slept off the first effects of the wine, woke to find "all the company were either sleeping or gone, except Agathon, Aristophanes, and Socrates, who alone remained awake and were drinking out of a large vessel, from left to right; and Socrates was arguing with them." Poor Aristodemus was a little unclear on the exact content of the argument but its substance was that "the fully skilled tragedian could be a comedian as well. While they were being driven to this, and were but feebly following it, they began to nod; first Aristophanes dropped into a slumber, and then, as day began to dawn, Agathon also." One must grant the tragedian Agathon a better capacity for wine than the great comedian Aristophanes but the entire scene is a victory for comedy. The only greater one would be if Socrates had argued for the superiority of tragedy while the comic poet Aristophanes slipped from the argument into drunken slumber.

2. COMEDY

In the last section I used the words tragedy and comedy mostly in the sense of divergent possibilities of drama. From here on the terms, while still including this meaning, will refer to much wider areas, to what is somewhat pompously termed the tragic sense and the comic vision. I admit, of course, that one can easily imagine two different dramatic or literary sequences one of which ends with the hero's death ("Good night, sweet Prince") and which is called *tragedy* and an opposite one which concludes with the hero's marriage ("Good night, sweet Princess") and is termed *comedy*. But beyond this somewhat feeble distinction I intend to view comedy and tragedy, in the words of Robert Martin, not as "forms of literature or genres, but formulations of modes of thought, attitudes toward the world, ways of coming to terms with the meaning of its triumphs and vicissitudes." And the question I wish to pursue was already broached in the preceding section. How does the tragic relate to the comic? Are they equal and alternating reactions to life or, if one is somehow more profound or inclusive, which response is best judged such? At least now.

A Narrow Escape into Faith

In a *Vogue* article for January 1951, Christopher Fry termed comedy "an escape, not from truth but from despair: a narrow escape into faith." He knew all too well that he was not advocating any Pollyanna attitude which ignored the stern reality of pain but he was holding "that there is an angle of experience where the dark is distilled into light: either here or hereafter, in or out of time." The brief article concludes with a refusal to maintain the superiority of comic perception over tragic vision. "I have come, you may think, to the verge of saying that comedy is greater than tragedy. On the verge I stand and go no further." But the article opened with a dream told him by a friend under the influence of ether and this parable probes over the edge that Fry himself would not transgress. He dreamt of a great book with alternating tragic and comic pages, and he turned them with mounting excitement to determine whether the last page which would furnish the meaning of life was to be tragic or comic. The final page contained one hundred words and "they were uproariously funny." He awoke immediately, and, still laughing, started to repeat that marvelous page. "It was then that the great and comic answer plunged back out of his reach." The ineluctable victory of the comic does not reside in having the last page or the best argument but in the possibility of losing the last page or forgetting the argument. It would have won just as much or even more, of course, if that last page had given a magnificent and irrefutable tragic meaning to our existence.

The New Sense of the Comic

The phrase is Wylie Sypher's and it can lead the discussion into its next point. He identifies our new sensitivity to the comic by noting that we have "been forced to admit that the absurd is more than ever inherent in human existence: that is, the irrational, the inexplicable, the surprising, the nonsensical —in other words, the comic."

An aside on the absurd. I am very deliberately using comedy rather than absurdity and I agree with Sypher that, as in the above quotation, the former swallows up the latter. If one has been taught or taken it for granted that reality evinces some great and overarching pattern of meaning established by God, chance, or evolution, and then has come to doubt the existence of such transcendental scenarios, it is easy to claim the world lacks meaning and is suffused with absurdity. Surely, however, Alain Robbe-Grillet is more accurate when he asserts that "the world is neither meaningful nor absurd. It quite simply *is*, and that, in any case, is what is most remarkable about it." My suspicion is that existential absurdity or absurd existentialism is but the dull receding roar of rationalism. Why should it be deemed absurd that what was never there was never there? Comic, by all means, but absurd protests too much.

Wylie Sypher will not say directly that comedy is more basic than tragedy but he will say this. "The comic now is more relevant, or at least more accessible, than the tragic." He knows quite clearly the savage malice that can be hidden (or shown) in laughter. Humans, too, know how to bare their fangs. Indeed the laughter of the ancients was mostly that of disdain and contempt, the disjunction of superiority and separation rather than the conjunction of equality and participation. Northrop Frye put it most succinctly. "One sometimes gets the impression that the audience of Plautus and Terence would have guffawed uproariously all through the Passion." But the sense of the comic which interests Sypher is not that of malicious disdain or mocking contempt. He is concerned with "the radiant peak of 'high' comedy [where] laughter is qualified by tolerance, and criticism is modulated by a sympathy that comes only from wisdom."

It is necessary to underline Sypher's analysis because it is in direct contradiction with one by Arthur Koestler which had appeared a few years earlier. For Koestler it is tragedy that establishes sympathetic participation "when sympathy and identification replace the feeling of superiority" and it is comedy that establishes "self-asserting superiority with its concomitant aggressive-derogatory tendency." I find myself very much on the side of Sypher in this debate. The drive of the tragic is towards separation, sympathetic of course, but sympathetic separation: There but for the grace of God go I. The thrust of the comic is to acceptance and participation: There by the grace of God go also I, and all of us. Koestler's view is the echo of a nineteenth-century prejudice. As Mikhail Bakhtin has said, "The bourgeois nineteenth century respected only satirical laughter, which was actually not laughter but rhetoric. (No wonder it was compared to a whip or a scourge.) Merely amusing, meaningless, and harmless laughter was also tolerated, but the serious had to remain serious, that is, dull and monotonous."

It is clear that laughter can be used to establish distance, separation, and superiority just as well as proximity, participation, and equality. Comic laughter partakes necessarily of this bifurcation or ambiguity. But at the heart of the comic for Sypher there is no laughter at all or at most a "mild inward laughter," a silent smile and that is why "the high comic vision of life is humane, an achievement of man as a social being." The comic, then, can exist with or without laughter. One might even propose an inverse relationship between them. The more profound and pervasive the comic perception, the less laughter ensues, but loud laughter will accompany the shallower manifestations of the comic phenomenon. With Wylie Sypher, then, we have moved to where we can say that "comedy seems to be a more pervasive human condition than tragedy."

Dark Comedy

Before continuing the argument, it is necessary to look at a most contemporary facet of our comic sensitivity, black humor or dark comedy.

W. H. Auden defined the comic in terms of painless contradiction and he insisted that it precluded real suffering or actual pain because such could only cause laughter to "human swine."

But Oscar Wilde once said that only a man with a heart of stone, could fail to laugh at the death of Little Nell. Are we human swine to find that funny?

In *Cat's Cradle* Kurt Vonnegut has the son of a jungle doctor tell what happened during an epidemic of bubonic plague. The "grisly tale" describes in specific detail how the "House of Hope and Mercy in the Jungle looked like Auschwitz or Buchenwald" with bulldozers stalling as the mounting death toll left too many corpses for them to shove towards a common grave. His father worked without sleep for many days but was unable to do very much to save the doomed patients. After one sleepless and fruitless night with every bed eventually holding a corpse the doctor suddenly started giggling. "He couldn't stop. He walked out into the night with his flashlight. He was still giggling. He was making the flashlight beam dance over all the dead people stacked outside. He put his hand on my head, and do you know what that marvelous man said to me? . . . 'Son,' my father said to me, 'someday this will all be yours.' "

It is such a story as this that I term dark comedy. If I find it funny, and I do, how do I not incur Auden's summary indictment?

Only a human swine laughs at plague victims or even at a story about them. We know and feel this proscription against laughter and, while plague is not comic, the awful truth is that the proscription itself can become comic. We always knew this from our inclination to laugh during solemn civil or ecclesiastical occasions but we also know it in tragic situations and even in cases of unmitigated horror. Presumably it is this which keeps us sane in such cases. I would also note that it took the reiterated concern of those "sleepless" nights of tending the plague-stricken to make very clear that the laughter was not at their pain but at this great stage of fools where the fullest, deepest truth is that, plague and all, it will belong some day to our children. Certain events are horrible and so are stories about them. Laughter at either event or story would be even more horrible still. But laughter at our inability to laugh is a narrow victory for the comic when faced with indescribable horror.

The Bias of Comedy

Nathan A. Scott has written a very instructive article combining that titular phrase with Fry's earlier one. He opposes Aristotle's claim that the tragic figure is better than we are and the comic protagonist below us. It is simply that the former is more extreme than we usually are and the latter more widely representative of our total humanity. "What the comic man cannot abide is the man who will not consent to be simply a man, who cannot tolerate the thought of himself as an incomplete and conditioned creature of a particular time and particular space." Scott develops his thesis by borrowing an incident from Aldous Huxley's essay "Tragedy and the Whole Truth." In Book 12 of the *Odyssey* Homer records the tragic fate of Odysseus's crew caught between the monster Scylla and the whirlpool Charybdis. When the survivors finally landed on the Sicilian shore they prepared supper and "when they had satisfied their thirst and hunger, they thought of their dear companions and wept, and in the midst of their tears sleep came gently upon them." Tragedy knows of Death and of Tears. But the Whole Truth knows of Death, Supper, Tears, and Sleep. It is this Whole Truth that Scott calls the comic vision. As with Fry, he does not want "to put comedy into the kind of competition with tragedy that would necessitate our opting for one against the other: so to pose the issues would, of course, entail an impossibly narrow kind of scholasticism." Neither do I wish or intend to opt for one *against* the other but neither do I see how one can avoid opting for one *above* the other. Tragedy can and does insist there is only Death and Tears. Comedy responds that there is Death and Supper, Tears and Sleep. Only loss of critical nerve can avoid the implications of these statements. If the same life or world or reality can be judged by some as tragic and by others as comic, then the latter has clearly won because it is already comic that the same events could be interpreted in such diametric opposition. Tragedy is swallowed up eventually in comedy. The sting belongs to tragedy but the victory to comedy.

The next step is to explore more fully this Whole Truth

which is the domain and victory of comedy. But before indicating the positive content of this wholeness, one negative reaction must be recorded.

Death unto Resurrection

Francis M. Cornford has shown how Attic comedy, and tragedy also, derived from ancient rituals intended to establish transition between old year and new, old king and new. These rituals afforded a rudimentary plot involving, for my present purpose, Birth, Struggle, Death, and Resurrection. Commenting on this, Wylie Sypher has concluded that tragedy developed only the first three movements of the ritual sequence but that comedy maintained the full ceremonial cycle. Which raises this question for Sypher. "Is this the reason why it is difficult for tragic art to deal with Christian themes like the Crucifixion and the Resurrection? Should we say that the drama of the struggle, death, and rising—Gethsemane, Calvary, and Easter—actually belongs to the comic rather than the tragic domain?" The answer to this question has to be affirmative, for clearly Bethlehem (birth), Galilee to Gethsemane (struggle), Calvary (death), and Easter (resurrection) is the Christian delineation of the full comic arc in the ancient Greek rituals. But two comments are in order. On the one hand, the Christian comedy leaves the world (birth, struggle, death) to tragedy and establishes comedy only in another and later world (resurrection). And on the other hand, this world of resurrection is itself divided into Hell and Heaven which means that tragedy and comedy are simply relocated elsewhere and frozen there into everlasting and unchanging actualities.

This is certainly *one* way of interpreting the Whole Truth which Scott cited as the gift of comedy. Tragedy gives us birth-struggle-death but comedy, the Whole Truth, adds to this, resurrection. I admit this is a form of comic wholeness but I reiterate the twin problematic just noted. I wonder if there is not another way to understand this Whole Truth in which birth-struggle-death can be seen from one viewpoint as tragic but which, this same reality but from another viewpoint, can be seen as comic. And this other viewpoint is what would then be called resurrection. I am not too terribly impressed with a comic victory that seems to occur as an afterthought or an appendix to a tragic sequence. *Anna Karenina* will not be changed from tragedy to comedy by having that train pull up in time. And the comic victory in Homer's Whole Truth was not that the dead arose but that the living slept.

3. PLAY

The Whole Truth which comedy whispers to our frightened or startled imaginations is that all is play. We are cats stalking with infinite ferocity a moving blade of grass. We are children preparing with infinite seriousness an eternal game of hide-and-seek. But first, back for a moment to Borges.

The Search of Averroes

In 1961 Borges gathered together a collection of poems, essays, and short stories and, declaring that "my preferences have dictated this book," he called it *A Personal Anthology*. Among them is one entitled "Averroës' Search." (I shall simplify his name, as in the later anthology, *Labyrinths*, to Averroes.)

The Arab philosopher's translation (of a translation) of Aristotle had ground to a problematic halt. "On the previous evening he had been nonplussed by two equivocal words at the beginning of the Poetics: the words *tragedy* and *comedy*. He had encountered them years before in the third book of the *Rhetoric*. No one within the compass of Islam intuited what they meant." Lacking any knowledge of theater, Averroes has no idea how to translate or even understand these enigmatic words. Chance now offers him two opportunities, but pride obscures the first and logic destroys the second one. Even as he ponders his problem noise draws him to the window where "some half-clad boys were playing." One, the minaret, allows another, the muezzin, to stand on his shoulders as he calls a third, the congregation, to prayer with the chant, "There is no god but God." The lowest of "the Peninsula's Moslem plebs" played out Islam's ancient destiny, but Averroes turned from the window congratulating himself on his library. He had eyes but did not see. Later that same evening he was listening to the experiences of the traveler Abulcasim at a dinner hosted by the Koranic scholar Farach. During after-dinner conversation Abulcasim, who had just returned from China, told them about a house he had visited in Canton with rows of balconies facing a terrace. "The people on the terrace played on drums and lutes, except for some score or so (who wore crimson masks) who were praying, swinging, and conversing. They suffered imprisonment, but no one could see the prison; they rode on horseback, but no one saw the horse; they fought in combat, but their swords were reeds; they died and then stood up again." Madmen, said his host contemptuously. Abulcasim tried to explain that they were "representing a story," they were like one who "shows a story instead of telling it." But Farach dismisses the subject amid general approval of his logical comment that one "speaker can relate everything, however complex it may be" so "there was no need for *twenty* people." Averroes, silent, had ears but did not hear.

The philosopher failed to understand the children's *play* in his patio or the traveler's *story* in the rose garden so he went home happily and translated with smug complacency, "Aristu (Aristotle) calls panegyrics by the name of tragedy, and satires and anathemas he calls comedies. The Koran abounds in remarkable tragedies and comedies, and so do the *mohalacas* of the sanctuary." Play is more primordial than either tragedy or comedy and both presume its possibility and its presence.

Borges intrudes on his own story at this point so that the form can make the same point as the content. How can he, Borges, understand Averroes any more than Averroes Aristotle? Widen the whole process: (1) You are reading (2) my comments on (3) a translation of (4) Borges's story about (5) Averroes's struggle to understand (6) a translation (7) of the text of Aristotle. Seven layers in all. Layers upon layers of solid play.

Homo Ludens

In the Foreword to his 1938 book, *Homo Ludens*, the Dutch scholar Johan Huizinga mentioned how his previous lectures on play and culture were usually understood to be concerned with play *in* culture whereas "it was not my object to define the place of play among all the other manifestations of culture, but rather to ascertain how far culture itself bears the character of play." Despite all this the English translation murmurs something about "the more euphonious ablative" and subtitles the work, "A Study of the Play-Element in Culture." A more accurate description would have been: A Study of Culture as Play.

He defines play as

> a free activity standing quite consciously outside "ordinary" life as being "not serious," but at the same time absorbing the player intensely and utterly. It is an activity connected with no material interest, and no profit can be gained by it. It proceeds within its own proper boundaries of time and space according to fixed rules and in an orderly manner. It promotes the formation of social groupings which tend to surround themselves with secrecy and to stress their difference from the common world by disguise or other means.

The chapters of the book argue that language, law, war, myth, poetry, philosophy, art, and indeed all cultural phenomena have unfolded *sub specie ludi*. It is a brilliant thesis but the argumentation suffers from a vacillation between the historical and the ontological, between proofs showing how culture came *from* play and is therefore somehow successive to it, and how culture arose *as* play and is therefore absolutely simultaneous with it. Note, for example, the two statements within the same paragraph that, "the spirit of playful competition is, as a social impulse, older than culture," but then the assertion that culture "does not come *from* play like a babe detaching itself from the womb: it arises *in* and *as* play, and never leaves it." This last sentence can be taken as the book's thesis, and one need not try to find some ancient moment when culture came forth from the womb of play. The thrust of the book is to define the human being as the one who plays, the one who always has and always will play.

Homo Ludens Revisited

The title comes from an article by Jacques Ehrmann written thirty years after Huizinga's classic study. It is clear, of course, that one could accept Huizinga's paradigm of the Player and yet disagree with this or that element included by him in his inaugural definition of play. But notice those two words, "ordinary" and "not serious," which he had placed in quotation marks in that definition itself. Ehrmann saw this and he also saw how often "real" and "reality" were placed in quotation marks by Huizinga in comparing the unreality of play with the reality of ordinary life. The nerve is exposed and Ehrmann presses on it relentlessly. And I think him absolutely correct.

A few sentences make his criticism quite precise. First, "if the status of 'ordinary life,' of 'reality,' is not thrown into question *in the very movement of thought given over to play*, the theoretical, logical, and anthropological bases on which this thinking is based can only be extremely precarious and contestable." Second, one cannot take this hypothetical ordinary reality "as a *given* component of the problem" and then go on blithely to "define play in opposition to, on the basis of, or in relation to this so-called reality." Third, and in conclusion, "This 'reality' which is considered innocent and behind whose objectivity some scholars sheepishly take shelter, must not be the starting point of any analysis but must rather be its final outcome." In plain language, Huizinga is still trapped in a dichotomized rationalistic world and cannot fully accept the radical implications of his brilliant intuition: reality is play, reality is make-believe, you make it to believe in and believe in what you have made.

Recall Huizinga's definition once again. Play was defined "as being 'not serious,' but at the same time absorbing the player intensely and utterly." One might well wonder what is serious if not that which absorbs one intensely and utterly. Play is terribly serious precisely because it absorbs the player intensely and utterly. Huizinga was not ready for the full conclusions of his fascinating insight but Ehrmann has formulated them most clearly. "Play is not played against a background of a fixed, stable, reality which would serve as its standard. All reality is caught up in the play of the concepts which designate it." Play has undermined and then absorbed reality. "In other words, the distinguishing characteristic of reality that it is played." Which still leaves us, of course, with good and bad play, absorbing and boring play, but only and always play.

The Play of World

Even before Ehrmann's critical evaluation of Huizinga's *Homo Ludens*, the German philosopher Eugen Fink had written that "in the history of thought, there have been those who have not only tried to conceive of the being of play, but also have dared an unheard of inversion of the process, concluding that the meaning of being springs from play." In his essay on "The Fearful Sphere of Pascal" Borges twice repeated the possibility that "universal history is the history of a handful of metaphors." And Fink had also noted this since speculation "is a conceptual formula of the essence of the world developed from a model within the world. The philosophers have used and perhaps abused models of this kind: Thales, of water; Plato, of light; Hegel, of the spirit; and the like." Play, then, is something easily visible within the world as game or as sport, but it can be taken speculatively as a metaphor or metonym for the whole, for world, and for reality itself. It is also obvious that play is a brilliantly inclusive metaphor since it can easily contain and include other models and metaphors by considering them as acts of supreme play. And notice that Borges did not say that the history of thought or of speculation is the history of a few great metaphors, but that "universal history" itself is such a sequence.

I have arrived, then, at this. To be human is to play. Our supreme play is the creation of world and the totality of played world is termed reality. This reality is the interlaced and interwoven fabric of our play. It is layer upon layer of solid and substantial play and in this and on this play we live, move, and have our being.

There are also two immediate ethical imperatives mandated by this acceptance. Kill not the play and kill not the player. Or, more positively, love the play and love the player. On this point I prefer Plato to Huizinga. The latter was quite willing to accept war as an example of play rather than, as I would hold, its perversion. Notice my italicized word in this quotation from his chapter on Play and War: "Needless to say, this archaic conception of war is soon *vitiated* by specifically Christian arguments advocating single combat as a means of avoiding unnecessary bloodshed." But Plato was wiser on this point, in the *Laws*.

I say that every man and woman ought to pass through life in accordance with this character, playing at the noblest of pastimes, being otherwise minded than they now are. . . . Now they imagine that serious work should be done for the sake of play; for they think that it is for the sake of peace that the serious work of war needs to be well conducted. But as a matter of fact we, it would seem, do not find in war, either as existing or likely to exist, either real play or education worthy of the name, which is what we assert to be in our eyes the most serious thing. It is the life of peace that everyone should live as well as he can.

Fink has reminded us of what another and even earlier Greek philosopher had said at the dawn of European thought. From *Fragment 52* of Heraclitus: "The course of the world is a child who plays at moving his pawns—a kingship of childhood." And in that later Galilean springtime another very great thinker warned us that unless we became as little children we would never enter the kingdom of God.

Breaks, Fissures, and Cracks

I have accepted play, well known to us in the microcosm of game and sport, as a supreme paradigm for reality. Reality as the interplay of worlds created by human imagination. It is on this basis that comedy will be understood throughout this book. Comedy is the conscience of play. The comic vision is our consciousness and awareness of the inevitability and ubiquity of play. Play is not in any way defined as the nonserious over against work, life, reality, or any other great pomposity as the truly serious. Play is strictly defined as make-believe and as-if. And it is the human propensity to forget, ignore, or even deny this ontological destiny of as-if that comedy can never allow. Whenever and wherever humans bypass this perspectival obligation and attempt to speak, act, or exist outside or apart from structures of the human imagination, comedy lifts its flaming sword and denies them any such passage or any such existence. Recall that terribly overworked comic example: the official in full-dress regalia steps towards the platform to receive his award and, slipping on the step, lands instead upon stern reality. We are amused. It was not that he was necessarily more serious than he should have been. He may even have been a most humble and well-loved person. But the fall is a comic reminder that *he and all of us there present* were playing out a scene and that it took only a slip to involve us all in a very different as-if, a very different play at being. To tell it like it is means to tell it like I-you-we-they see it. Comedy is the conscience and consciousness of the inevitability of play.

Two quotations from Borges will illustrate this point. In collaboration with his long-time friend, Margarita Guerrero, he wrote a new preface for the expanded 1967 edition of their joint work *The Book of Imaginary Beings*. This fantastic zoology includes such inventions as the biblical Behemoth and the celtic Banshee but the preface opens with a sentence which questions the very distinction between fantasy and reality. "The title of this book would justify the inclusion of Prince Hamlet, of the point, of the line, of the surface, of n-dimensional hyperplanes and hypervolumes, of all generic terms, and perhaps of each one of us and of the godhead. In brief, the sum of all things—the universe." But the second quotation is even more significant. The first one had reminded us that we can never get outside the human imagination, not in art, not in philosophy, and not in science. Put most simply "imaginary beings" is a redundant description which includes our universe itself and all its contents including ourselves. The second citation not only repeats this inevitability of playful imagination, but it also underlines the necessity of keeping this ineluctability openly conscious and freely acknowledged. Borges concluded his 1939 essays on "Avatars of the Tortoise" with this assertion.

"The greatest sorcerer [writes Novalis memorably] would be the one who bewitched himself to the point of taking his own phantasmagorias for autonomous apparitions. Would not this be true of us?" I believe that it is. We (the undivided divinity that operates within us) have dreamed the world. We have dreamed it strong, mysterious, visible, ubiquitous in space and secure in time; but we have allowed tenuous, eternal interstices of injustice in its structure so we may know that it is false.

The dream of world is play and the tenuous interstices, the breaks, the fissures, the cracks, the surprises, are the gift of comedy lest we ever forget that, as Yeats put it,

> Death and life were not
> Till man made up the whole,
> Made lock, stock and barrel
> Out of his bitter soul,
> Aye, sun and moon and star, all
> And further add to that
> That, being dead, we rise,
> Dream and so create
> Translunar Paradise.

Bitter soul, maybe, but playful and comic soul, certainly. It may also be necessary to revise that equally famous line from Yeats's *Autobiographies* and write it now like this: After us the Comic God.

The Range of Comic Play

Comedy, then, is the epiphany of play. Comic play is play made manifest. And the range of comic play extends from the scatological to the eschatological. I would even suspect that the greatest comedy is that which fuses together "low" and "high" comedy, scatology and eschatology into a transcending unity. Think of Falstaff as a character or of Rabelais as a writer. I would also suspect, as intimated earlier, that laughter is at its most boisterous in the scatological and at its most silent in the eschatological. But, together, scatology and eschatology unite to remind us that we all have the same end.

On scatology: I depend once again on Wylie Sypher's excellent study. "At the bottom of the comic scale—where the human becomes nearly indistinguishable from the animal and where the vibration of laughter is longest and loudest—is the 'dirty' joke or the 'dirty' gesture." There is nothing, of course, dirty or obscene in itself. It is our taboos, customs and morals that accept or forbid certain words or deeds in certain places or situations. And immediately we invent jokes to remind us that all such proscriptions are acts of play. We make them up and, necessary as many of them are, even more necessary is the comic laughter that reminds us of their relativity. "Yet laughter at the obscenest jest forever divides man from animal, because the animal is never self-conscious about any fleshly act whatever." But we are self-conscious because clothed/unclothed flesh reminds us that we are all in costume and always playing one role or another. In the world is in the play. Animals, on the other hand, do not have to disrobe in either bathroom or bedroom.

On eschatology: and from the Bible to Beckett. The term is very well known in biblical studies. Scholars usually distinguish an earlier prophetic eschatology from a later apocalyptic eschatology along the following general and controversial lines. The prophets were quite willing to write in retrospect the scenario of God's activity with his Chosen People, but they were more diffident with the future. There the vision was usually of destruction so catastrophic as to involve *an ending of world* as Israel had known it. Example would be the destruction of the Northern Kingdom by the Assyrians in the eighth century or the devastation of the Southern Kingdom by the Babylonians in the sixth century B.C.E. Whatever lay beyond such cataclysm, be it small or great, good or bad, would be like another world. But always, of course, the prophets were talking of this earth since they had absolutely no conception of another life anywhere else. With the apocalyptists, however, a very radical change is introduced. Here one attempts to read the great scenario laid out by God in Heaven. One envisages a complete and usually imminent *ending of this world* which includes destruction of Israel's enemies and the relocation of the persecuted saints to eternal happiness with God. I would describe such eschatology, be it prophetic or apocalyptic, as tragic eschatology. World ends with both bang and whimper.

This present book will involve a different view of eschatology than either of the tragic vistas in the Hebrew Bible or the Christian New Testament. I am interested in comic eschatology which I see as much more basic and fundamental than any such tragic ending of world. The supreme act of play is world and when one player forgets or denies such playful creativity, it is necessary for another player to disintegrate world by comic eschatology and to renew thereby the springs of play and the relativity of world. Comic eschatology restores world *sub specie ludi*. Two quotations, one from and the other on Samuel Beckett, can serve to indicate the outlines of such comic eschatology.

Arsene, a character in Beckett's *Watt* has established a hierarchy of three grades of laughter.

> The bitter laugh laughs at that which is not good, it is the ethical laugh. The hollow laugh laughs at that which is not true, it is the intellectual laugh.... But the mirthless laugh is the dianoetic laugh, down the snout—Haw! so. It is the laugh of laughs, the *risus purus*, the laugh laughing at the laugh, the beholding, saluting of the highest joke, in a word the laugh of laughs—silence, please, at that which is unhappy.

For myself, as distinct from Arsene, I do not find that the *risus purus* is down the snout but, apart from this divergence in taste, I find this a perfect description of the laughter of comic eschatology. But I also find that the silent laughter of comic eschatology is what binds us all most democratically together. It is the glad acceptance of a common fate. And, as such, it is love made visible. The second quote is from an article by Stanley Cavell on "Ending the Waiting Game." He is commenting on one of the characters in Beckett's *Endgame*.

> Suppose what Hamm sees is that salvation lies in the ending of endgames, the final renunciation of all final solutions. The greatest

33 Comedy and Transcendence

endgame is Eschatology, the idea that the last things of earth will have an order and a justification, a sense. That is what we hoped for, against hope, that was what salvation would look like. Now we are to know that salvation lies in reversing the story, in ending the story of the end, dismantling Eschatology, ending this world of order in order to reverse the curse of the world laid on it in its Judeo-Christian end.

I take that paragraph as a most exact definition of what I term comic eschatology, and I presume that its appropriate laughter is the *risus purus* of silence. I sense that *risus purus* is a degree of laughter which an author such as Marie Collins Swabey can never quite face up to in her book *Comic Laughter: A Philosophical Essay*. "In our opinion, if experience is not to dissolve into a welter without distinctive meaning, reference, or definition of terms, both logical laws and moral standards must remain effective in the realm of the comic." Comedy must be carefully inoculated before it is safe even to investigate its processes! For my part I much prefer that vision of salvific comedy where, as Wylie Sypher has it, "we must stand on the brink of Nonsense and Absurdity and not be dizzy."

4. STRUCTURE

I use the term structure as it has developed along the critical trajectory extending from Slavic formalism in the first decades of this century to contemporary French structuralism.

A System of Transformations

Probably the clearest definition is that given by Jean Piaget.

As a first approximation, we may say that a structure is a system of transformations. Inasmuch as it is a system and not a mere collection of elements and their properties, these transformations involve laws: the structure is preserved or enriched by the interplay of its transformation laws, which never yield results external to the system nor employ elements that are external to it. In short, the notion of structure is comprised of three key ideas: the idea of wholeness, the idea of transformation, and the idea of self-regulation.

Structured Play

Think now of any game you know quite well. Is it not a microcosmic totality, a *whole* closed off by mutually established *rules*, but within which a very great variety of different options or *transformations* are always possible? It should also be underlined that this closure of game does not strike us as a negative liability but as a positive challenge. What is most clear, however, is that there is no play without structure and that Homo Ludens is necessarily Homo Structurans, the Player always plays in and with structure. The French philosopher Jacques Derrida has already made this conjunction of structure and play in a paper on the theoretical bases of the anthropology of Claude Lévi-Strauss. He is talking about language but the comment is true of all human play as field. "This field is in fact that of freeplay, that is to say, a field of infinite substitutions in the closure of a finite ensemble." This is a good definition of all human play and it differentiates itself only according to the rules established for this form of play as over against that, for example, for art or philosophy or science. And "infinite substitutions" is not an exaggeration for even if exactly the same transformational possibility is repeated a second time, that very secondness changes the option.

In the Beginning

I am presuming in all this that it is the playful human mind which establishes and imposes structure. I do not think of structures as already existent in "reality-out-there" and discovered or acknowledged by our obedient minds. What is there before or without our structured play strikes me as being both unknowable and unspeakable. Call it chaos if you will but remember by that very naming you have drawn "it" inside the structure of human language. The French theologian Georges Crespy started an article on structuralism with the phrase, reminiscent of Genesis 1:1 and John 1:1, "In the beginning was the structure. It was everywhere in the world and the world had been organized by it." He finds such structure in the minerals, the crystals, the vegetable and animal kingdoms, and, finally, in human rhetoric. It is a beautiful thought but unfortunately the opposite may be just as true. I would prefer to reverse his paragraph and say: In the beginning was human rhetoric and it proceeded forthwith to structure all things. In other words, I prefer the following from Kurt Vonnegut's *Breakfast of Champions* as an example of human play with structures and in structures. "I wrote on the tabletop, scrawled the symbols for the inter-relationship between matter and energy as it was understood in my day: $E=Mc^2$. It was a flawed equation, as far as I was concerned. There should have been an 'A' in there somewhere for *Awareness*—without which the 'E' and the 'M' and the 'c', which was a mathematical constant, could not exist." In fact one might rewrite that famous equation more fully and more accurately and with a quite deliberate acronym: $HA(E = Mc^2)^{fn}$ where HA is human awareness (structured play) and fn means for now.

The Ritual Process

Once again, however, it is all too easy for human beings to forget or deny the playfulness of such structures. And when one denigrates such creative play, which is our very ontological lifeblood, comedy must assert itself in the comic play of anti-structure. This is what Victor W. Turner's book *The Ritual Process* with its subtitle "Structure and Anti-Structure" demonstrates so admirably. Turner is an anthropologist who ranges widely into literature, philosophy, and religion the better to understand the data afforded by his fieldwork among the Ndembu of northwestern Zambia. His thesis is that *communitas*, which we could define as authentic or ideal human community, involves an interplay of structure and antistructure. He moves convincingly from the Zambezi Flood Plain to the Haight-Ashbury and from Zen Buddhism to Franciscan poverty to explain this distinction. Under structure he includes "rituals of status elevation" those well-known rites of transition which structure the important stages of both individual and communal existence. But where many anthropologists stop at this point, Turner introduces, as antistructure, "rituals of status reversal." These are rituals in which weak, inferior, marginal, or liminal individuals or groups are allowed at certain times to humiliate both verbally and actually those structurally above them in the standard hierarchy. This phenomenon of deliberate antistructure is found in ritual, in literature, and in the history of religion. In ritual, for example, the Barotse drummers tossed from the royal barge those nobles who had offended them the previous year. In literature, "Members of despised or outlawed ethnic and cultural groups play major roles in myths and popular tales as representatives or expressions of universal-human values. Famous among them are the Good Samaritan [etc.]." In religion, there is the marginality of the beat generation and the liminality of the various millenarian movements. Turner sums up his thesis as follows: "Communitas breaks in through the interstices of structure, in liminality; at the edges of structure, in marginality; and from beneath structure, in inferiority." To this point I am in complete agreement with Turner's analysis. But then there seems to be, as so often in these dangerously subversive areas, a certain loss of nerve.

It is clear that rituals of status elevation create and reinforce structural order and hierarchy but Turner concludes that so do rituals of status reversal: "they reaffirm the hierarchical principle. . . . they underline the reasonableness of everyday culturally predictable behavior between the various estates of society." I agree, of course, that status reversal rituals do not destroy the structural hierarchy of society. But I cannot agree that societies with strongly entrenched reversal rituals are not changed by such a presence. Do we really believe that the *Apo* ceremony of the northern Ashanti of Ghana which allows before each new year eight days of complete license to mock and criticize superiors does no more than reinforce structural hierarchy? I prefer to interpret this ritual dialectic as the necessary human *interplay* of structure and antistructure, of elevation and reversal, which reminds us continually that our structures are both absolutely necessary and completely relative. In this sense, then, I am in complete agreement with Turner's final conclusion that "the liminality of status reversal may be compared to comedy, for both involve mockery and inversion, but not destruction, of structural rules and overzealous adherents of them."

Turner's interpretation of this ritual dialectic can be complemented with a work such as Mikhail Bakhtin's fascinating study of *Rabelais and His World,* a work of Russian formalist criticism written in 1940. He talks of the "double aspect of the world and of human life [which] existed even at the earliest stages of cultural development. In the folklore of primitive peoples, coupled with the cults which were serious in tone and organization were other, comic cults which laughed and scoffed at the deity ('ritual laughter'); coupled with serious myths were comic and abusive ones; coupled with heroes were their parodies and doublets." But later a very serious change takes place in this dialectic. "At the early stages of preclass and prepolitical social order it seems that the serious and the comic aspects of the world and of the deity were equally sacred, equally 'official.'" This official dualism later gave way to an official-serious and an unofficial-comic dichotomy. "All the comic forms were transferred, some earlier and some later, to a nonofficial level." Thus, for example, "the official feasts of the Middle Ages, whether ecclesiastic, feudal, or sponsored by the state, did not lead the people out of the existing world order and created no second life." So, over against this official seriousness, in which we already recognize our buttoned-down modern mind, authentic human festivity went elsewhere to play and to celebrate irreverence. It was in the medieval carnival spirit that we find this "characteristic logic, the peculiar logic of the 'inside out' (*à l'envers*), of the 'turnabout,' of a continual shifting from top to bottom, from front to rear, of numerous parodies and travesties, humiliations, profanations, comic crownings and uncrownings. A second life, a second world of folk culture is thus constructed; it is to a certain extent a parody of the extracarnival life, a 'world inside out.'" But its primary characteristic is not negative but positive, the sheer, shining joy of playful celebration and all-encompassing laughter.

5. LITERATURE

Comedy manifests play. Play is structure. Hence, comic anti-structure. But language is the structure of structures. Hence, literature.

Language as Play

The father of modern linguistics is the Swiss theoretician Ferdinand de Saussure. Yet in order to illustrate his brilliantly original distinctions between *langue* (a language) and *parole* (an utterance) in human speech, or signifier (vocal sound) and signified (mental image) in the linguistic sign, or synchrony and diachrony in the historical existence of any system, or paradigmatic substitution and syntagmatic succession in the formation of grammatical sentences, he could find no better analogy than chess. "But of all the comparisons that might be imagined, the most fruitful is the one that might be drawn between the functioning of language and a game of chess. In both instances we are confronted with a system of values and their observable modifications. A game of chess is like an artificial realization of what language offers in a natural form." I would add that the reason language and chess can be so fruitfully compared is that both are magnificent examples of structured play. Indeed I would even go so far as to suggest that language is simply our supreme play.

Language as Supreme Play

De Saussure himself saw linguistics as part of a wider study which he proposed to call "*semiology* (from Greek *sēmeîon* 'sign'). Semiology would show what constitutes signs, what laws govern them. Since the science does not yet exist, no one can say what it would be; but it has a right to existence, a place staked out in advance. Linguistics is only a part of the general science of semiology." He also hinted, however, that linguistics is a privileged part of semiology since "linguistics *can* become the master-pattern for all branches of semiology although language is only one particular semiological system" (my italics).

The French linguist Emile Benveniste stated flatly, however, that linguistics has much more than a privileged possibility within semiology or semiotics because "the configuration of language determines all semiotic systems." Roland Barthes has gone even further in his *Elements of Semiology* by "inverting Saussure's declaration: linguistics is not a part of the general science of signs, even a privileged part, it is semiology which is a part of linguistics: to be precise, it is that part covering the *great signifying units* of discourse." Language is the supreme structure, the structure of structures, and, at minimum, we must agree with Robert Scholes that, "Language is so central to human communication that no other meaning-system can manage without its aid." At maximum, it may well be the paradigm for all other structures, the very model of semiology.

The Conscience of Language

What does all this contribute to our present discussion? As the supreme act of human play language can also and easily become the supreme enemy of human play. Indeed it can play with us and persuade us that it imitates a "reality-out-there" rather than our creating reality with and in it. It is here that the destiny of literature appears most clearly, and, once again, I am depending heavily on the work of Roland Barthes. In the Theme section at the front of this book I quoted his literary credo demanding the simultaneity of semiology and semioclasm, or of what Victor Turner would have called structure and antistructure. Two other quotations from Barthes may clarify his ethical demand that iconoclasm be built intrinsically and self-consciously into our literary structures. In 1961 in answer to a questionnaire for the Parisian periodical *Tel Quel* he discussed the meaning of literary realism. It is a long argument and I give it in full as indication of its importance for my general thesis.

In other words, in relation to objects themselves, literature is fundamentally, constitutively unrealistic; literature is unreality itself; or, more exactly, far from being an analogical copy of reality, *litera-*

ture is on the contrary the very consciousness of the unreality of language*: the "truest" literature is the one which knows itself as the most unreal, to the degree that it knows itself as essentially language. . . . Realism, here, cannot be the copy of things, therefore, but the knowledge of language; the most "realistic" work will not be the one which "paints" reality, but which, using the world as content (this content, moreover, is alien to its structure, i.e., to its being), will explore as profoundly as possible the *unreal* reality of language.

The second quotation is from his book *On Racine* and it indicates how the unreal reality of language threatens the real unreality of world. "To write is to jeopardize the meaning of the world, to put an *indirect* question that the writer, by an ultimate abstention, refrains from answering." Literature, then, should be the conscience of languge and, if it too has failed its destiny at times, it seldom got away with it for too long. Or, whatever happened to the realistic novel?

What is happening here before our eyes is the death of mimesis. When reality was thought of as existing out-there by itself prior to and independent of our knowledge and our language, this latter could be considered as groping more or less effectively to describe that reality, and one could then claim that literature was where it was grasped the best of all. (Nobody seemed at all disturbed by the fact that *reality* was a word and was therefore already inside our language to begin with.) It is this linguistic bad faith that Barthes is calling to account and he is defining literature precisely as that which reveals to language its own art-ificiality and un-reality. But he also insists that the "content," the "world," the "reality" is known to us only as the *"unreal reality"* (or real unreality?) of language. We know reality only in language.

Defamiliarization

Two examples from Russian formalist criticism can illustrate all this and possibly indicate as well how residual realism can weaken a challenging literary theory.

Victor Shklovsky of the St. Petersburg "Society for the Study of Poetic Language" proposed "the device of making it strange" or defamiliarization as the principal aim of literature. Victor Erlich describes this technique: "Rather than translating the unfamiliar into the terms of the familiar, the poetic image 'makes strange' the habitual by presenting it in a novel light, by placing it in an unexpected context." I consider defamiliarization to be a crucially important insight, but in reading Shklovsky's 1917 article "Art as Technique" I find it somewhat unclear whether literary art must make strange the external *object* (the world out-there) so that we can see it afresh or make strange *language* (the world in-it) so that we can hear it anew. He says, for example, that, "Habitualization devours works, clothes, furniture, one's wife, and the fear of war.... And art exists that one may recover the sensation of life; it exists to make one feel things, to make the stone *stony*. The technique of art is to make objects 'unfamiliar,' to make forms difficult, to increase the difficulty and length of perception because the process of perception is an aesthetic end in itself and must be prolonged." Or again, "After we see an object several times, we begin to recognize it. The object is in front of us and we know about it, but we do not see it—hence we cannot say anything significant about it. Art removes objects from the automatism of perception in several ways." But then when one is all set to read this as simply a new permutation of the mimetic fallacy, one finds this, and in italics: "*Art is a way of experiencing the artfulness of an object; the object is not important.*" For myself, and to avoid any ambiguity, I would rephrase: Art is a way of experiencing the artfulness of language; the object is linguistic. I prefer to think that defamiliarization is necessary so that we may see the world-in-language more openly and more honestly. Literature makes language strange not the better to recognize world, but the better to acknowledge language.

A second example is the distinction between story (*fabula*) and plot (*sujet*) suggested by Boris Tomashevsky of the Moscow Linguistic Circle. Meir Sternberg has summed up the difference: "The *fabula* of the work is the chronological, or chronological-causal sequence in which these motifs may be arranged; while the *sujet* constitutes the actual arrangement or presentation of these motifs in the work itself." At first glance this distinction of story and plot seems eminently correct. One can imagine dozens of different plots within the same story: start at the end and flash back, etc. There is only one problem and that is not with plot but with story. What is this *unplotted story* which serves as secure chronocausal base? Is it itself not just another possibility of plot even if one which strikes our own or another's historical situation as being unplotted? In other words the play of plotted against unplotted story is simply a relative one; there is only plotted story. And the function of the multitudinous plots is to make the inevitability of plot apparent and not to work variations around some central, enthroned, and unplotted story.

The New in Literature

Literature renews language as play, our most marvelous play, our play of play, but still and always play. Literature is ever old and ever new because it must always make strange our language and must never let that strangeness lose its compelling challenge. As T. S. Eliot said in his essay on "Tradition and the Individual Talent," the arrival of any new work of art forces the entire ideal order which was there before it to alter itself, to rearrange itself "and so the relations, proportions, values of each work of art toward the whole are readjusted." This simultaneous change of the entire ideal unity of art by the introduction of "the really new" has another facet ignored by Eliot. As we suddenly begin to see all preceding art in the light of the new arrival we become conscious of the *arti*ficiality of the entire process and are forced to ask ourselves if there is any alternative to such *arti*ficiality. So it is that literature, as verbal art, both renews our language and also renews itself in phoenixlike continuation. The structuralist critic Tzvetan Todorov has reiterated this theory of Eliot even more forcefully. "*Every* work modifies the sum of possible works, each new example alters the species." He distinguishes popular or mass literature from artistic literature by this criterion. Only "a text which produces a change in our previous notion" of literature is artistic literature. In other words, new literature makes strange both our current language and our older literature. Literature reveals as play both language and itself. And there is no way out.

(There is still hope for all this despite, and maybe even in, college freshman composition. Two quotes from a 1974 manifesto by Richard A. Lanham in *Style: An Anti-Textbook*. To begin with, "Poetry is, after all, language in a state of play." And thus the crucial question: "To what degree does a writer acknowledge his style *as a style*? To what degree are we to *feel* the style as such? To what degree, that is, does the style realize itself as opaque, as—the enemy of clarity—a style to be looked *at* rather than *through*?")

Style is the enemy of both clarity and unclarity because it is the echo of a higher law. As Borges also knows: "This will be our destiny—to give ourselves to syntax, to its treacherous linkage, to imprecision, to perhaps, to the exaggerated emphasis, to buts, to the hemisphere of lies and shadows in our sayings."

6. Transcendence

With Rudolf Otto I name the referent of transcendental or mystical experience as The Holy. This is what strikes us as both absolutely fascinating and equally terrifying. Both, and both together, and each precisely as the other. Think, on a less absolute or total level, of the fascinated fear or fearful fascination engendered in an audience by the tightrope walker far above their heads and without a safety net. Or take up any dangerous sport for yourself. And I admit, in passing, that I find this name more interesting than, say, Ultimate Concern which strikes me as a feeble submission to a humanism ultimately inhuman.

In bringing together comedy and transcendence, the comic and the Holy, I must begin with the negative, with what I do not mean, and only then pass on to the positive in their relationship.

A Great and Secret Plan

The negative. Consider four assertions. First, the Holy has a great and secret master plan for the universe in process of gradual but inevitable realization. Second, this overarching scheme is known only to chosen initiates. Third, alternatively, the cosmic plan is a mystery and thus inscrutable to all human intellect. Fourth, the Holy has no such plan at all and that is what is absolutely incomprehensible to our structuring, planning, ordering human minds. I admit immediately that the fourth proposition represents my own position. But I also know that the first assertion, accompanied by some variation of the second or third, has a long and most distinguished history.

Biblical exegetes working with both Old and New Testament books of the Christian Bible have been especially prone to discover the lineaments of this divine plan revealed in their texts and have given it a special name redolent of its origins in German scholarship. They call it *Heilsgeschichte* or history of salvation. They were not incorrect in discovering it there since even more brilliant minds had gone to the trouble of hiding it there for them to find. Let those who love the story and think there is no alternative to it pay full degree of tribute to such creative genius. To the Yahwist, the Deuteronomist, and the Chronicler, for example, who forged the vagaries of Israel's history into the unfolding of a transcendental drama. And to Luke who, among those who have ever told story anywhere, must never be underestimated.

(It used to be fashionable to say that Paul invented Christianity. Now we know better. Luke invented Christianity and in the process invented Paul as its propagator. It is amusing to find scholars who usually tend to radical and systematic doubt on the historicity of his *Acts of the Apostles* accept as critically certain the presence of Paul at Corinth in the years 51 to 52 because Luke has him appear before Seneca's brother, L. Junius Gallio, in Acts 18:12, and we know his proconsular dates from a Delphic inscription. All this really proves of course is that Luke knew about Gallio but not when Paul was at Corinth.)

It might be useful to write as the epigraph if not the epitaph of *Heilsgeschichte*, especially when accompanied by archeological or historical discoveries, this dialogue between Borges and a Madrid journalist on his 1945 story "The Aleph." The journalist: "Ah, . . . so the entire thing is your own invention. I thought it was true because you gave the name of the street." And Borges: "I did not dare tell him that the naming of streets is not much of a feat." Borges has also argued, as quoted by D. E. Turner, that, "the lack in the Koran of such a typical feature of the landscape as the camel proves its authenticity." And there is also the serene warning of the biblical God that: My ways are not your ways. The naming of streets, or towns, or cities, or battles, or kings, or whatever history can verify, is not much of a feat. It is time, then, to challenge biblical eschatology with the iconoclasm of comic eschatology.

I have already described comic eschatology as the ending of endgame, the silent laughter at our invention of a divinity whose coherent plan is moving, imminently or distantly, towards some final consummation. Comic eschatology laughs at the idea of a final ending which, by teleological retrojection, might clarify and justify all preceding events.

Kurt Vonnegut, once again, has already thrown into high relief these facets of comic eschatology. He has this to say of the start of *Heilsgeschichte* in his novel *Cat's Cradle*. God has just created Adam. "Man blinked. 'What is the *purpose* of all this?' he asked politely. 'Everything must have a purpose?' asked God. 'Certainly,' said man. 'Then I leave it to you to think of one for all this,' said God. And he went away." And on the continuation of *Heilsgeschichte*, this, from *The Sirens of Titan*. Rumfoord, on the planet Titan, explains to Chrono the secret coherence of all our human history as seen in galactic perspective. "The sickening thing is this: *Everything that every Earthling has ever done has been warped by creatures on a planet one-hundred-and-fifty thousand light years away.* The name of the planet is Tralfamadore. How the Tralfamadorians controlled us, I don't know. But I know to what end they controlled us. *They controlled us in such a way as to make us deliver a replacement part to a Tralfamadorian messenger who was grounded right here on Titan.'*" Later on, the Tralfamadorian messenger opens and reveals the "message . . . that I have been carrying for almost half a million Earthling years— the message I am supposed to carry for eighteen million more years." The message is: "Greetings." Comic eschatology is the ending of Game and therefore of Endgame but the establishment of games and therefore of endgames.

One final word, still on the negative side. I have no intention and less desire to add to Aquinas's five a sixth proof for the existence of God, a proof, that is, from play. I do not see reality, world, ourselves as the play of God the Player. At times Borges seems to envisage some great and secret order behind the universe as, for example, in the text chosen as epigraph for this First Variation where he talks of "God's secret dictionary" and "the impossibility of penetrating the divine scheme of the universe." And in his poem "Chess" he talks directly of God as Player:

> The player, too, is captive of caprice
> (the sentence is Omar's) on another ground
> crisscrossed with black nights and white days.
>
> God moves the player, he, in turn, the piece.
> But what god beyond God begins the round
> of dust and time and dream and agonies?

I do not imagine the Holy as Player unless I take this in oxymoron as the Player-without-Rules or the Play-without-Structure, or, in a word, the Holy as Wholly Other.

The Comic and the Holy

Positively, then, what is the relationship of comedy and transcendence, of the Comic and the Holy?

Conrad Hyers has written a very provocative book on *Zen and the Comic Spirit* in which comedy is taken to mean cosmic iconoclasm as in the present book. He acknowledges "the widespread taboo against associating the comic too closely with the sacred," which is radically overthrown in the comic iconoclasm of the Zen imagination. "There has probably never been a religious movement more sweepingly iconoclastic than Zen.

Idols of every sort are relentlessly and mercilessly smashed: not only the ego and its desires and attachments, but scripture, doctrine, tradition, meritorious works, liturgy, prayer, gods, miracles, Bodhisattvas, and even the Buddha himself. Much of the humor in Zen is therefore iconoclastic in character; for before true liberation can occur, all idols must be overturned, or stood upside down. Anything, however holy, is potentially an idol; therefore anything is a legitimate object of laughter." I agree completely with this analysis and would only add that Zen, Judaism, and Christianity, save when they lose their souls, that is, their sense of humor, find in comedy and iconoclasm the only gateway to transcendence.

All of which Søren Kierkegaard said of religion in general and of Christianity in particular well over a hundred years ago. In his *Concluding Unscientific Postscript* he said that, "There are thus three spheres of existence: the aesthetic, the ethical, and the religious. Two boundary zones correspond to these three: irony, constituting the boundary between the aesthetic and the ethical; humor, as the boundary that separates the ethical from the religious." Earlier in the work he had explained how humor itself will not allow an individual to remain in the boundary zone of itself but will push one towards the religious. "The comic is in general present everywhere, and every type of existence may at once be determined and relegated to its specific sphere by showing how it stands related to the comical. The religious individual has as such made the discovery of the comical in the largest measure, and yet he does not regard the comical as the highest, for religiosity is the purest pathos. But if the individual regards the comical as the highest, then his own comic consciousness is *ipso facto* lower; for the comical always lies in a contradiction, and if the comical itself is the highest, there is lacking the contradiction in which the comical consists, and in which it makes its showing." Once again the comic trap is sprung: it is not possible to accept the ubiquitous inevitability of comedy without also invoking the Holy for whom all must appear as wholly other than it does for us. The religious individual has broken through to the silence on the other side of comedy.

Biblical Laughter

One example from a biblical story which stands at the very source of both Judaism and Christianity. Consider the laughter of Sarah and Abraham. In Genesis 21:6–7 a son is born to the aged couple. His name, Isaac, is etymologically explained: "And Sarah said, 'God has made *laughter* for me; every one who hears will *laugh* over me.'" Earlier in Genesis 18:12–15 God and two attendants appeared in human guise and promised Abraham that Sarah would bear him this son. "Now Abraham and Sarah were old, advanced in age; it had ceased to be with Sarah after the manner of women. So Sarah laughed to herself." When God hears the laughter and remonstrates with her Sarah denies the laughter. And God: "No, but you did laugh." Even earlier, however, in 17:16–17 there is another account of this from a different source. This time it is a direct apparition by God to Abraham and once again the child, Isaac, is promised: "I will bless her, and moreover I will give you a son by her; I will bless her, and she shall be a mother of nations; kings of people shall come from her.' Then Abraham fell on his face and laughed, and said to himself, 'Shall a child be born to a man who is a hundred years old? Shall Sarah, who is ninety years old, bear a child?'" And Abraham tries to change the subject.

When Paul had to explain to the Romans how Abraham was saved by faith before the Cross of Christ had come he insisted that it was because he believed in a God "who gives life to the dead and calls into existence the things that do not exist" (4:17). Laughter is not, of course, mentioned. And yet it is precisely the combination of laughter and faith that is the only adequate human response to the Holy. One laughs and one believes and if it is not laughable it should not be believable. Abraham and Sarah are the parents of faith for both Judaism and Christianity and they are also the parents of laughter.

With this most auspicious beginning the God of the Hebrew imagination was declared to be fundamentally and intrinsically comic. Existent but aniconic, named but unmentionable, present but invisible. I have always wondered what Titus really thought as he stormed through the empty Holy of Holies in Israel's burning Temple. Did he catch an echo, even if only the faintest echo, of the silent laughter of Israel's ancient God?

And did the Corinthians appreciate the dark laughter of the Cross when Paul wrote them concerning it: "For the foolishness of God is wiser than men, and the weakness of God is stronger than men" (1 Cor. 1:25)?

At the Limits of Language

When comedy ensures that language, rendered strange by literature, is seen most openly and acknowledged most freely as structured play, the narrow gate to transcendence has been opened. It is this intuition that holds together the various quotations cited in my Theme section at the start of this book.

The text of Susan Sontag there is taken from her article on "The Aesthetics of Silence," and I wish to cite it more fully here. Were it seemly I would like to have quoted it in full. "Traditionally, it has been through the religious vocabulary with its meta-absolutes of 'sacred' and 'profane,' 'human' and 'divine' that the disaffection with language itself has been charted. In particular, the antecedents of art's dilemmas and strategies are to be found in the radical wing of the mystical tradition." This tradition, she maintains, includes Zen, Taoist, Sufi, and Christian texts. Among Christian writers think, for example, of Dionysius the Areopagite, Jakob Boehme, Meister Eckhart, or the author, appropriately anonymous, of the *Cloud of Unknowing*. Across all the world's great religions, the mystical tradition had always played at and with the limits of language. "But, in our time, the most striking development of such ideas have been made by artists (and certain psychotherapists) rather than by the timid legatees of the religious traditions."

It is because I agree so completely with these citations that I bring together in this book an ancient Palestinian mystic and a contemporary South American poet. I am not interested in their personalities nor their authorial intentions but in what they have done within language and against its manifold possibilities. I am especially interested in the comic eschatology that informs their serene and iconoclastic spirits. I accept both Jesus and Borges as Magistri Ludi, this Galilean and this Argentine parabler with, in Emir Rodríquez-Monegal's phrase, their "fragmentary and minimal art." And if I have termed one a mystic and the other a poet, it may well be that each is both and the difference only in emphasis. In their study of South American writers Luis Harss and Barbara Dohmann called Borges "a mystic Montaigne," and Jorge Rodrigo Ayora finished his Vanderbilt doctoral thesis on Borges with this comment. "Thus, by means of paradox and parable, of stylistic and structural surprise, of imagination and scholarship, of the succinct that explodes with huge implications, Borges has constructed a very peculiar universe in which he keeps up the questioning. And in so doing he leaves a heritage of beauty, complexity, and transcendence."

But above all else, if I may borrow both a title and subtitle from Jerzy Peterkiewicz, Jesus and Borges are poets at the limits of language, parablers who can evoke for us the other side of silence. Together they invite us to rejoice anew in the play of language as Rilke has done in his "Sonnets to Orpheus,"

> Welcome to all we have snatched like this
> from doubt, the mouths re-endowed with power
> of speech, after knowing what silence is.

And I presume that the word "after" is the single most important one in that entire quotation.

Postlude: The Secret of the People

I finally come back to the question posed in the Prelude to this First Variation: What is the Secret? I am aware of Robert Lima's warning that "the nature of the tale is such that it invalidates any definition of the 'secret'" and I intend not so much to solve it a to enlarge its scope.

Ronald Christ asked Borges the solution to the riddle when he was in New York in 1968 "and I knew, at once, my error."

Borges replied, "I'd like to keep you guessing one more day." Pressed on the following day he confided in a whisper that the secret rite was sexual intercourse as the means of propagation. "When I first heard about this act, when I was a boy, I was shocked, shocked to think that my mother, my father had performed it. It is an amazing discovery, no?" One recalls immediately what Borges makes Emma think in his 1948 story "Emma Zunz": "She thought (she was unable not to think) that her father had done to her mother the hideous thing that was being done to her now."

Even allowing for Borges' deliberate playfulness in handling Christ's question, I must admit that I am not terribly impressed by a Society whose Secret nobody knows at birth but everyone knows by death. I am much more impressed by the suggestion of James Irby that the secret involves a biological and a metaphysical pole, that human continuity is established by an act of secret biology but also by a much more secret act of metaphysical creation. Parents create children and bring them into a world they have already created to receive them and if the former act is temporarily a secret for all, the second one is permanently a secret for many.

Two justly famous stories by Borges support this expanded concept of the Secret as biological-metaphysical creation. Both were written in 1940 and contained in the first volume of his short stories issued in 1941. In "The Circular Ruins" a priest-magician-father has a purpose which "was not impossible, though it was supernatural. He wanted to dream a man: he wanted to dream him with minute integrity and insert him into reality." When he finally succeeded he gradually accustomed "my son . . . the child I have engendered" to reality and before he sent him away "he instilled into him a complete oblivion of his years of apprenticeship." The only difference between his dream son and any normal child was that the priest-magician-son was impervious to fire. Later the father is himself surrounded and unharmed by a raging forest fire. "With relief, with humiliation, with terror, he understood that he too was a mere appearance, dreamt by another." Carter Wheelock's book on Borges *The Mythmaker* has already drawn attention to this fire as that which renews the phoenix, the "continual world-dissolution (burning, which is the method of the self-destroying, self-regenerating Phoenix)." This is the biological pole of the Secret known only to the sectarians of the Phoenix. We are born in the dreams of each other.

The second story is "Tlön, Uqbar, Orbis Tertius," a work of consummate and brilliant artistry. (How little Borges has changed can be seen by comparing this first story from his first collection of 1941 with the last story from his most recent collection, "Dr. Brodie's Report," in the 1970 anthology with the same title.) In this story it is no longer a question of one man secretly dreaming another into existence and inserting him into reality but of a vast secret society composing an artificial world to impose it gradually upon our own planet. "In the early seventeenth century . . . a secret and benevolent society . . . arose to invent a country." This nonexistent country was to be known as Uqbar. But when the secret society arrived in America in 1824 "the ascetic millionaire Ezra Buckley" argued that it was absurd to invent only a country and proposed the invention of a planet. Buckley dedicated all his wealth to the production in forty volumes of the *First Encyclopedia of Tlön*, a project which took almost one hundred years to finish. When this complete edition was delivered to the three hundred or so members of the secret society in 1914 the next stage of the plot was set. A complete revision of the encylcopedia was planned but "in one of the languages of Tlön." This revision would be termed Orbis Tertius and it would be its role to infiltrate the planet Earth. Indeed one might consider Orbis Tertius as the new name of our planet as it was gradually taken over by Tlön. And, of course, this usurpation is effected in Tlönistic manner so that our minds gradually accept its concepts and these ideas are then concretized in objects. Slowly but surely, from 1942 onwards, *objects* from Tlön began to appear on our planet. But here a very strange phenomenon occurs. In order to ensure victory Tlön had to modify its original theoretical foundations and begin "exhibiting a world which is not too incompatible with the real world." Originally, Tlön had been a construct of pure and absolute *play* in which philosophical idealism (materialism was a heresy so unthinkable as to be almost inexpressible) had triumphed completely. For example, "there are no nouns in Tlön's conjectural *Ursprache*" and, on the other hand, their philosophies are treated like nouns in the northern hemisphere. They are simply uncountable. But as Tlön adapts itself or is adapted in its absorption of Earth it becomes a rigid, monolithic and dogmatic structure of total and impeccable order. In the story's postscript, dated 1947, that is seven years after its first readers were actually perusing it, Borges describes the victory of Tlön. "Almost immediately, reality yielded on more than one account. The truth is that it longed to yield. Ten years ago any symmetry with a semblance of order—dialectical materialism, anti-Semitism, Nazism—was sufficient to entrance the minds of men. How could one do other than submit to Tlön, to the minute and vast evidence of an orderly planet? It is useless to answer that reality is also orderly. Perhaps it is, but in accordance with divine laws—I translate: inhuman laws—which we never quite grasp. Tlön is surely a labyrinth, but it is a labyrinth devised by men, devised to be deciphered by man." And so gradually we become Orbis Tertius as the vast and harmonious inevitability of Tlön's usurpation gains momentum and we are all being slowly prepared for the arrival, in another hundred years, of the Second Encyclopedia of Tlön, in one hundred volumes. Then, and completely, "The world will be Tlön." And by then we shall have completely forgotten that, before contamination with our earth, Tlön would have been a fascinatingly marvelous place on which to live/play.

The Secret is play, the entire realm of play from the biological to the ontological, from our birth in the play of sex to the world's birth in the play of imagination, from "The Circular Ruins" to "Tlön, Uqbar, Orbis Tertius." Frances Wyers Weber has articulated this Borgesian play most clearly in an article on "Borges's Stories: Fiction and Philosophy." What Borges does is to create imaginary worlds but not in an exercise of the imaginary over against the real. "Instead of establishing an entirely independent realm of game and conjecture, Borges's fiction–making irradiates its ambiguity and playfulness to all the activities of mind." This statement at the start of the essay is matched by another summary at the conclusion. "It is this consciousness of fabrication that we must persistently maintain in relation to our verbal constructions, whether prose or poetry, science or fantasy. And Borges's fictions, in playing out a drama of postulation and dissolution, illustrate what should be the ironic and playful ideal of all mental activities."

The necessity and ubiquity of play is the Secret of the People, and its great and universal symbol is the Phoenix, ever ancient and ever new. But unless play is kept self-conscious both in its relativity and in its necessity, any form of it and most especially any larger form will degenerate into the totalitarian tyranny of Orbis Tertius. So, as play extends from the biology of sex to the ontology of world, there must also exist its conscience, comedy, expanding correspondingly from the scatological to the eschatological. Or, as Weber, put it: "All representations of the world, whether given as 'fact' or fiction, should display an equal awareness of their tentative nature."

Second Variation:
Form and Parody

> Literature is a game with tacit conventions; to violate them partially or totally is one of the many joys (one of the many obligations) of the game, whose limits are unknown.
>
> So perhaps what is important in any tradition is what is rejected or changed. Is that possibly the meaning of a tradition?—that things should be modified.
>
> Jorge Luis Borges

In the preceding Variation, I defined comedy as the conscience of play, as our iconoclastic consciousness of the inevitability and ubiquity of play. The Second and Third Variations will study the comic and iconoclastic eschatology of Jesus and Borges in their parodies of forms of language and modes of writing which had taken on almost absolute normative value within their respective traditions. Forms of language and genres of communication are the iron girders of world and their parody is always eschatological in its full implications.

1. ICONOCLASM

Mention has already been made of the aniconic God of Israel, and I must return to this supreme and most devastating model of iconoclasm to introduce this Variation.

No Graven Images

It is not surprising to find that ancient Israel prohibited images of foreign gods lest such deities impugn the absolute sovereignty of Yahweh. What is surprising, however, is the total prohibition against any images of Yahweh, God of Israel. This injunction against plastic images of Yahweh is usually associated with the religious genius of Moses. The reason for this decree is because "you saw no form on the day that the Lord spoke to you at Horeb out of the midst of the fire." This is Deuteronomy 4:15, and the allusion to the theophany at Mount Sinai explains why the Israelites must not "act corruptly by making a graven image for yourselves, in the form of any figure" (4:16). The proscription is specified in great detail: *no* figures, neither male nor female, neither beast nor bird nor reptile nor fish, and not even the celestial spheres themselves (4:17–19). In Isaiah 40:12–19 this absolute decree against graven or plastic images of Yahweh is given a philosophical rather than an historical basis. "To whom will you liken God, or what likeness compare with him" (40:18). The idol or the image is the work of a skilled craftsman be it in silver and gold for the rich or in "wood that will not rot" for the worshiper of more limited means. But what image on earth can possibly portray the God who made the earth, asks Isaiah. Hence the supreme challenge of Israel's God is this: " 'To whom will you compare me, that I should be like him?' says the Holy One" (40:25). No images, not only because none were ever seen but also because none are ever possible.

From Images to Words

There was already a problem evident in that quotation given above from Deuteronomy 4:15 where "you saw no form" but heard what "the Lord *spoke* to you." Was that consuming fire whence spoke the Lord strong enough to burn all plastic images but not all verbal forms? Might there not be an idolatry of forms and images made by minds just as easily as there could be such for forms and images made by hands? Why mock the craftsman skilled in silver and gold and not mock the artisan skilled in form and genre? Bereft by divine command of plastic images, Israel's destiny turned to verbal forms, and with that most magnificent vocation went hand-in-hand a most paradoxical temptation. What if the aniconic God became trapped in icons made of language, fashioned skillfully in the forms, modes, and genres of human speech?

There is some evidence in our extant texts that this problematic possibility was known to authors in the Hebrew Bible itself. Since the general trend of this canonical collection is to integrate divergent traditions into more or less harmonious unity, very careful attention must be paid to those works which resist or even negate this process of retroactive unification.

Two examples will suffice for now, others will be discussed in later sections, and together these will cover the major strands of Israel's traditions. The present ones are the traditions of Law and of Wisdom, the legal and sapiential traditions.

First, the legal traditions and their comic questioning by the book of Ruth. In the restoration of Israel following the Babylonian Exile fidelity to God's Law was to be the foundation of the renovated community. Indeed, the decree of the Persian monarch Artaxerxes given in Ezra 7:11–26 repeatedly emphasized this point and concluded that, "Whoever will not obey the law of your God and the law of the king, let judgment be strictly executed upon him, whether for death or for banishment or for confiscation of his goods or for imprisonment" (7:26). A crucial point in this legal purification was the prevention of marriage between Jews and foreigners and even the enforced divorce of any such marriages which had already occurred. Both Ezra and Nehemiah lament most vehemently these mixed marriages which they held as breaches of God's law. Officials inform Ezra of what has happened. "For they have taken some of their [foreigners'] daughters to be wives for themselves and for their sons; so that the holy race has mixed itself with the people of the lands." His reaction in Ezra 9:2–3 is immediate. "When I heard this, I rent my garments and my mantle, and pulled hair from my head and beard, and sat appalled." The reaction of Nehemiah is quite similar although he prefers the hair of others to his own. In Nehemiah 9:23–25: "In those days also I saw the Jews who had married women of Ashdod, Ammon, and Moab. . . . And I contended with them and cursed them and beat some of them and pulled out their hair." But the stern conclusion of both Ezra and Nehemiah is compulsory divorce from all foreign wives.

Against all this stands the serene message of the pastoral idyll in the book of Ruth. This book may once have been no more than an example of divine reward for familial fidelity and as such it would have ended at 4:17a. The German scholar Otto Eissfeldt, for example, has argued that 4:17b–22 is an addition which turns Boaz and Ruth into the greatgrandparents of David, King of Israel. At the moment I am concerned with the story in this final form concluding with the Davidic genealogy in 4:17b–22. When this very beautiful short story is read against the legal demands of Ezra and Nehemiah its satirical polemic is as devastating as it is muted, for Boaz and Ruth, ancestors of King David, are a Jew and a Moabitess. Naomi had emigrated from Bethlehem to Moab and her sons had married Moabite women. After the sons' deaths Naomi returns to Bethlehem and Ruth insists on accompanying her. "Where you go I will go, and where you lodge I will lodge; your people shall be my people, and your God my God; where you die I will die, and there will I be buried" (1:16–17). Later Ruth, coached carefully by her mother-in-law, marries the rich landowner Boaz of Bethlehem. Their first child is "Obed; he was the father of Jesse, the father of David" (4:17b), and their genealogy is repeated in greater detail in 4:18–22. Throughout the story we are never allowed to forget that Ruth is a foreign wife. There is constant repetition of Moab, and she is repeatedly referred to as Ruth the Moabitess.

The parodic point is quite clear. What would have happened to King David if Boaz the Jew and Ruth the Moabitess had obeyed the later regulations of Ezra and Nehemiah? The book of Ruth does not destroy the books of Ezra and Nehemiah. But by questioning their absolute decisions it warns that God must not be trapped in the idolatry of legal tradition, even of legal tradition couched as God's decree.

A second example, from the wisdom tradition and its comic questioning in the book of Ecclesiastes. Proverbial wisdom is a notoriously ambiguous operation. For every "Two heads are better than one" there is always another "Too many cooks spoil

59 Form and Parody

the broth." As Israel's wisdom tradition moved from collections of independent proverbs to maxims clustered around the same subject and on into much longer and more integrated sapiential essays, the problem of making it all cohere pressed ever more insistently upon its thought. What was the divine purpose behind it all and, most especially, what and where were the divine sanctions that controlled virtue and vice, rewarding the good and punishing the wicked. Was it all as sublimely simple and consistent as Proverbs 10:3 had proposed? "The Lord does not let the righteous go hungry, but he thwarts the craving of the wicked." Were goodness and happiness, evil and suffering actually and always such iron correlatives?

Ecclesiastes did not find it so and he satirized the wisdom tradition in fragmentary aphorisms whose form and content alike denied the claim of total understanding. The more gentle satiric comment of Ruth upon the legal tradition here gives way to a bitingly ironic commentary on the wisdom tradition. If Solomon stands as the symbolic head of this latter tradition, Ecclesiastes will don the mask of Solomon and declare the claims of wisdom to be vanity because he knows, "How the wise man dies just like the fool" (2:16). And he insists that good people suffer, bad people prevail, and even if the reverse were always true, it would be but a relative punishment since death alike awaits them both. All of which, and much more, adds up to this. "I saw all the work of God, that man cannot find out the work that is done under the sun. However much man may toil in seeking, he will not find it out; even though a wise man claims to know, he cannot find it out" (8:17). But if the human mind will cease the claim to have worked it all out and to have grasped the meaning of it all, it then becomes possible to accept this limited life as the gift of God and to enjoy it before the face of the Giver. First, however, one must see "that under the sun the race is not to the swift, nor the battle to the strong, nor bread to the wise, nor riches to the intelligent, nor favor to the men of skill; but time and chance happens to them all" (9:11). Only then is one ready to accept as sufficient that, "it is God's gift to man that every one should eat and drink and take pleasure in all his toil" (3:13). Ecclesiastes does not preach against wisdom but against wisdom's claim to understand and to find meaning and purpose only in that understanding. Israel's sapiential tradition and Greece's tragic vision both agreed that no matter how awful the horror might be, it would be still more horrible if it lacked logical causality and divine inevitability. But the dark and enigmatic insight of Ecclesiastes insists that God cannot be caught in the nets of Wisdom any more than in the nets of Law.

No Graven Words

If the name of Moses is synonymous with the prohibition against graven images, against images of God in gold and silver, it is Jesus who issues the most magisterial warning against graven words, against images of God in form and genre. Think for a moment of those great traditions which form the very substance of the Hebrew Bible: Cult, Law, Wisdom, Prophecy, and Apocalyptic. I have just argued that the Hebrew Bible itself contained comic and satirical warnings against the idolatrous possibilities of the legal and wisdom traditions. In the Third Variation I shall return to this point with the book of Jonah as a comic parody of the prophetic tradition and, in a minor key, of the cultic one. But it is most especially with Jesus that we find comic injunctions against *all* these traditions and especially against his contemporary apocalyptic traditions. The content of Jesus' message is a comic eschatology of forms and genres. In his teachings the aniconic God of Israel escapes not only wood and stone, silver and gold, but also eludes the images of human imagination and the forms of human language. Jesus represents the full flowering of Israel's aniconic faith, the consummate creativity of Israel's iconoclastic imagination. As such he offers to both Judaism and Christianity a challenge always accepted by both their mystics and always suspected by both their ministers.

2. Genre

What I have said concerning Jesus is, of course, programmatic and will have to be substantiated throughout this book.

But here is what is most interesting in all this. The linguistic challenge of Jesus to his tradition is remarkably similar to the perennial iconoclasm of literature within its own tradition. And it is here that Jesus and Borges meet on common ground. So before turning to these twin parablers, a few words on the formal iconoclasm of literature itself.

Literature as System

In discussing literature in the First Variation I cited the agreement between the classical critic T. S. Eliot and the structuralist critic Tzvetan Todorov on literature as an "ideal order" (Eliot) where "each new example alters the species" (Todorov). It is as if all the chairs and all the space in the auditorium were occupied so that one new arrival involves a total reorganization of those already present. It is of course this new arrival which stops the entire proceedings from becoming static, lifeless, and boring since all those in the audience face not the empty stage but rather the closed door. This subversive advent is necessary because without it the established forms and genres of a period's language and style would become absolutes and their frozen immobility would effectively hide the foundations of play on which and in which they operated.

This necessary clash of forms and genres takes place within the possibilities of literature seen as a closed system. The adjective closed has here no connotation of privation or loss but has rather the exhilarating challenge of spatial or temporal closure involved in any human game. In his book *The Anxiety of Influence* Harold Bloom studied the relationship between poets *as* poets and he concluded "that the meaning of a poem can only be a poem, but *another poem,—a poem not itself.*" It is only in such dialectic of poem and other-poem, and even or especially when the latter never knew the former, that literature reveals itself openly as play, as not only playing with language but also playing with itself.

Generic Transformations

None of this is particularly new even if more critics record the fact than face fully its implications. Murray Krieger has reminded us of the paradox at the heart of literature. First, literature is "a medium that is at war with its role, language that subverts the normal behavior of language in order to attain the character of sacred communion which symbolism has lost in the secular world." Second, not only at war with its role, but "the medium is at war with itself in literature." And Claudio Guillén talks in *Literature as System* of Cervantes as one involved in "an actual dialogue with the generic models of his time and culture," and here, of course, the lance prevailed.

With Guillén we can imagine a vast and interlocked system of genres and agree that "as they change they affect one another and the poetics, the system to which they belong, as well. Although Genres are persistent models, because they have been tested and found satisfactory, it has been generally known since the Enlightenment . . . that they evolve, fade, or are replaced." My own suspicion is that there is a literary ecology at work in this process and that genres are never so moribund that a poet cannot surprise us again with their revival in new guise.

Alastair Fowler has written an article on "The Life and Death of Literary Forms" in which he suggests three major phases of generic development. He considers these as "organic and invariable in sequence, though development need not go beyond the first or second." The first phase is *Creation* when "the genre-complex assembles, until a formal type emerges." One can allow for a high degree of sophisticated unawareness being present at this phase. It is probably clearer to speaker and hearer or to writer and reader what is *not* being done than what is being created at this point. The second phase is *Imitation* where there is the creative handling of "a form that the author consciously bases on the earlier primary version." Finally, there is *Recreation* (both senses of the word) "when an author uses a secondary form in a radically new way. The tertiary form may be burlesque, or antithetic, or symbolic modulation of the secondary." Thus this final phase may move towards either Parody or Symbol, the genre may beget an antigenre or it may be combined with earlier genres. In either case its temporary ascendancy is temporarily transcended. It is also clear that, as indicated by my choice of descriptive titles for the three phases, there is a cyclical or spiral relationship between *Recreation* and *Creation*. The arrival or creation of a new genre will usually be a direct or indirect recreation by parody or allegory of other and earlier genres.

It is at this point of generic recreation that the linguistic creativity of Jesus and Borges will be compared in this book. But I would insist that both poets are intensely aware of what they are doing. It is never an attack on Genre A in order to establish the monolithic replacement by some Genre B. It is the relativity of any genre including necessarily their own antigenres that is at stake. Jesus learned it from the aniconic God of Israel and Borges learned it from the history of literature.

I would recall one other point from the Russian formalist Victor Shklovsky whose principle of defamiliarization appeared at an earlier stage of the discussion. Shklovsky also insisted that literature must underline the techniques by which it was making language strange. In his 1921 article on *Tristram Shandy* he said of Sterne that "it was characteristic of him to 'lay bare' his technique" and he concluded that this work "is the most typical novel in world literature." It is obvious that such polemical enthusiasm is not to be taken literally. If everyone wrote like Sterne there would be immediate need for anti-Sterne novels. But the basic point is valid and important. Literature must make language strange and also lay bare the technique whereby it effects such a process. At least that is its destiny.

With this background I shall now turn to compare Jesus and Borges in terms of comic eschatology and radical generic parody.

3. Law

Ezra and Nehemiah proposed a case: If you have married a foreign wife, you must immediately divorce her. Ruth proposed an anticase, a case parody, a legal satire: If Boaz had divorced Ruth, what would have happened to David? We have already seen this, and it is in this antitradition that a first example of Jesus' language can be placed.

Case Law

There is a collection of case laws in Exodus 20:22–23:33 which scholars usually call "The Book of the Covenant." Case or casuistic law can be easily distinguished from apodictic law in that the former presents a case or situation which may even have multiple subsituations ("if/whenever . . . then . . . but if . . . then . . .") while the latter is an unqualified absolute ("Thou shalt" or "Thou shalt not"). In reading through these case laws one is immediately struck by their sound common or uncommon sense. They are clear and sensible and helpful. Take, for example, Exodus 21:12–14, "*Whoever* strikes a man so that he dies shall be put to death. *But if* he did not lie in wait for him, but God let him fall into his hand, *then* I will appoint for you a place to which he may flee. *But if* a man willfully attacks another to kill him treacherously, you shall take him from my altar, that he may die." This is our distinction between accidental homicide and premeditated murder. It also recognizes that the dead person's kin may be less interested in this distinction than is God, and so places of refuge are necessary for tempers to cool and explanations or judgments to be made. The content of all these cases is eminently reasonable and there is also a more or less standard format. First, the case or situation is established by opening with "if" or "whoever" or "when" etc. Second, this situation is developed in a balanced diptych of protasis and apodosis. Third, the protasis or first part describes what the offender has done to the offended party. Fourth, the apodosis or second part tells what the offended party, be it individual or society, can and should do to the offender. So the protasis is offender to offended and the apodosis is offended to offender.

At the time of Jesus it was the Pharisees who had fallen heir to this magnificent tradition of case law based on the covenantal relationship between Yahweh and Israel. Christian polemics and Christian chauvinism have called them hypocrites, which simply proves that Christians can also be liars. The Pharisees were careful and prudent moral guides helping people to live according to the demands of God's law in new and changing situations. They were case moralists whose authority over the people at the time of Jesus is sufficient evidence of just how good they were and how helpful they were held to be.

Case Interpretation

Take, now, that most famous injunction of Jesus on turning the other cheek. The case is given in a series of three in Matt 5:39b–41 of which Luke 6:29a–29b has kept only the first two. It is because two different evangelists interpret the same source that we can now separate their editorial commentary from the core sayings which go back to Jesus himself.

The set of three parallel cases is given thus in Matt 5:39b–41: "But if any one strikes you on the right cheek, turn to him the other also; and if any one would sue you and take your coat, let him have your cloak as well; and if any one forces you to go one mile, go with him two miles." The version in Luke 6:29 has only two cases and their formulation is terser: "To him who strikes you on the cheek, offer the other also; and from him who takes away your cloak do not withhold your coat as well."

I wish to differentiate as precisely as possible what comes from Jesus in all this and what stems from evangelical creativity. Jesus gave a set of three cases extremely parallel in form and expanding in content from one's person (cheek) to one's possessions (coat) to one's time and labor (miles). The trilogy format is quite customary with Jesus as indeed with many oral poets in the Western tradition. This general phenonemon has been known at least since the turn of the century and Axel Olrik has claimed that, "The Law of Three extends like a broad swath cut through the world of folk tradition, through the centuries and millennia of human culture. The Semitic, and even more the Aryan culture, is subject to this dominant force." Jesus' set of three was, therefore, a harmonious unit both in form and content and indeed the folkloric threesome stands symbolically for any much larger or longer series of such cases.

What exactly did the two evangelists do with this series of three linked cases? In themselves the cases are concrete, specific, radical, and extreme. Both internal changes and especially external comments from both Matthew and Luke seek to mute and interpret this paradoxical formulation of Jesus.

First, internally. Matthew softens the second case by changing it from violent theft as in Luke 6:29b ("takes away your cloak") to juridical suit in his 5:40 ("sue you and take your coat"). Luke, on the other hand, softens the first case by changing "right cheek" from Matt 5:39 to "cheek" in his own 6:29a. Presumably a blow on one's *right* cheek would have to be delivered by the striker's right hand and would therefore have to be a backhanded one and so a most insulting blow. And Luke omitted that third case which is probably the hardest of them all. If a (foreign?) military force conscripts you to carry materials for them one mile, go also a second mile with them. Recall the case of Simon of Cyrene forced to carry the cross of Jesus in Matt 27:32.

Second, externally, and once again one senses that the evangelists are somewhat uneasy with these radical statements and wish to change them back into more helpful normalcy. Indeed, even before they commented on the series, the common source used by both writers had itself done so. This common source added on a generalizing conclusion which attempted to make Jesus' three cases sound rather like almsgiving. In Matt 5:42, with much the same in Luke 6:30, it had added: "Give to him who begs from you, and do not refuse him who would borrow from you." The difference in form and in content is quite clear and it is unlikely that anyone will be convinced that Jesus was just talking about aid and alms in those three preceding cases. Matthew himself interprets Jesus' set with his preliminary 5:39a, "do not resist one who is evil." This may be sound advice but it is not what Jesus said. He advised not only not to resist evil *but even to join in one's own despoiling*. And Luke terminated the unit with the Golden

Rule in 6:31, "And as you wish that men would do to you, do so to them." Once again this is extremely good advice but it is not clear how it interprets or even comments on Jesus' sayings. The general conclusion from all this is that the three sayings or cases in Matt 5:39b, 40, 41 go back to Jesus, and the tradition, both *before* and *in* Matthew and Luke, attempted to explain them as practical almsgiving and nonresistance of evil. But what exactly did Jesus' original threesome actually mean?

Case Parody

My own theory is that Jesus' set of three situations represents case parody, a deliberate comic subversion of the wise and prudent necessity of case law. It is clear that they have the standard format of case law as outlined earlier: opening in a hypothetical situation; protasis of offender to offended; and apodosis of offended to offender. But the parody appears in the content within this set format, and most especially in the ridiculous discrepancy of the usual measured harmony and appropriate balance between protasis and apodosis. The protasis of Jesus' cases always opens like good, solid, helpful case law concerning acts of personal attack and aggression: If someone does this to you . . . We await legal advice or moral decision in the apodosis. We imagine such conclusions as, in a biblical seven ranging from extreme negative to extreme positive: kill him, maim him, strike him, flee him, forget him, forgive him, love him. This spectrum of apodictic possibilities, extending from the negative ethics of Lamech in Genesis 4:23 to the positive ideal of Luke 6:35, has one point in common. It is in continuity with the protasis and, easy or difficult, bad or good, lethal or loving, it could not be termed ridiculous or nonsense. But instead of such apodoses, Jesus gives us a strange injunction to join in our own despoiling. This apodosis does not tell what the offended can or should do to the offender but advises the former to go over to the side of the latter. The alternatives were there in language and were not used. Unless one invokes authorial incompetence, the conclusion must be that they were not used because they were functionally inapplicable. Jesus is not offering case law, however ideal or radical, but he is challenging his legal tradition, like the book of Ruth before him, in the form of case parody.

This single example must suffice for here since it is clearly a classic instance. No doubt there are many other case parodies and legal satires in our texts and these will also have to be separated just as carefully from framing commentary which mutes their comic challenge and attempts to turn them into that which they originally subverted, back, that is, into case law itself.

Beyond Morality

What exactly does case parody accomplish? I would take as epigraph for this section the claim of Albert Camus that, "We live for something that goes farther than morality. If we could only name it, what silence!"

There was nothing wrong with Hebrew or Pharisaic case law and there is no possibility, at least that I can envisage, of decent human existence without legal principles and case laws. But precisely because case law is so important, case parody is the more deeply imperative. Law can so easily be absolutized either in the name of raw human force or in the more subtle name of divine commandment. Case parody reminds us that our best and most necessary laws are still but legal play, our laws and therefore our play. It points us back to the silence that precedes and surrounds them.

An example of this more fundamental morality, of what is before and beyond morality, may be seen in the *Letter on Humanism* of Martin Heidegger. In this work of 1947 he was responding to three questions posed by the French philosopher, Jean Beaufret. The second query was how one might make clear and precise the relationship between ontology and ethics. Heidegger answers with Aristotle's story about the visitors who came to see the Greek philosopher Heraclitus. They were surprised and probably disappointed to find the great thinker in so mundane an occupation as warming himself at the stove. He invited them in with the reassurance that, "Here too there are gods present." As Heidegger interprets this it indicates that the thinker must warm himself at the divine fire before and if he is to have anything to say. So he concludes that the most original and fundamental ethics is, as the word *ēthos* ("dwelling") shows, man's abiding with Being. In Heidegger's words: "More essential than any establishment of rule is the abode in the truth of Being." And this, I would suggest, is the ontological function of case parody. It stops and arrests the forward development and expansion of case law by satirical laughter. This is not done, however, in order to furnish law with new insights or directions contained within these sardonic aphorisms. Rather does its parody turn case and law and rule backwards towards their source and, by blocking any literal interpretation of its own dictum as ridiculous, remind us over and over again that to abide with the Holy is more fundamental than any case law and is itself original ethics and fundamental morality. It is also much more dangerous.

4. PROVERB

In the language of Jesus the comic subversion of law by case parody finds a close parallel in the comic subversion of wisdom by counterproverb, that is, of proverbial aphorism by paradoxical aphorism.

Proverbial Wisdom?

André Jolles was a Dutch historian of art and literature who taught in Germany and published there in 1930 a book entitled *Einfache Formen* which one might translate as *simple,* or better, *basic* forms of speech. His nine basic forms are Legend, Saga, Myth, Riddle, Proverb, Case, Memoir, Tale, and Joke. Concerning his discussion of proverb the American critic Robert Scholes has written that "there is more of the oracular and unfathomable in proverbs than he seems to allow. Brought together, 'Look before you leap' and 'He who hesitates is lost' can hardly function as guides to conduct. They suggest, in fact, that empiricism itself cannot advise us very helpfully about our actions. The behaviorist can tell us everything except how to behave." Proverbial wisdom is, as I noted earlier, replete with this type of admonitional contradiction. In other words, proverbial wisdom *as a whole* is a most paradoxical guide.

When one reads through the biblical book of Proverbs, however, one is struck by the general good sense of its injunctions and is seldom made aware of the enigmatic possibility of lining up the proverbs in parallel columns where each one is contradicted by another. The point of all these proverbs is for the reader to "keep my commandments and live" (7:1). But what if there were individual proverbs which brought forcibly to one's attention the paradoxical contradiction between many proverbial admonitions? What if there was paradox *in* a proverb and not just *between* proverbs?

Paradoxical Aphorism

The presence of hyperbole in the language of Jesus is very well known. There is, for example, the famous comment in Mark 10:25 that, "It is easier for a camel to go through the eye of a needle than for a rich man to enter the kingdom of God." And while hyperbole is language well on its way to paradox and is already straining the complacency of more conventional proverbial wisdom, it is paradoxical aphorism as antiproverb that concerns me at the moment. Two examples will suffice and in both cases it is amusing to watch the evangelists and even some modern English translators trying to mitigate and interpret the radical nature of the *double* paradoxes presented to them by Jesus.

The first example is the saying, "To him who has will be given; and from him who has not will be taken away." There is no such version as this anywhere in our extant texts but I would argue that it is absolutely necessary to posit it hypothetically in order to explain the divergent readings presently available in three different sources: in the common source for Matt 25:29 and Luke 19:26 (known to scholarship as Q); in Mark 4:25 which is the source for Matt 13:12 and Luke 8:18; and in Thom 41.

As I have reconstructed the saying of Jesus above it is in perfect parallel format. The mind grinds agonizingly to a halt before its double paradox and stutters to itself: but if you

71   Form and Parody

have, what can be given, and if you have not, what can be taken away? And the tradition which preserved the logion in three different sources did its very best to make interpretive sense out of it. And as we shall see some translators added in their own helpful changes as well.

Matt 13:12 and 25:29 must be credited with "solving" the first half with an additional phrase, italicized: "For to him who has will [more] be given, *and he will have abundance* . . ." The "more" is not in the Greek but has been slipped into the protasis by recent English translators. (Translators like their work to sound sensible.) But the second half, being even more enigmatic than the first, encouraged everyone in the tradition to interpretive enthusiasm. Q commented, as now in Luke 19:26, "but from him who has not, *even what he has* will be taken away." And the same change is in Mark 4:25. Thom 41 made a different one, "and whoever does not have, from him shall be taken *even the little which he has*." Finally, Luke 8:18 offers a more subtle explanation, "and from him who has not, *even what he thinks that he has* will be taken away." The process whereby ancient writers and modern translators have tried to explain away the stern intransigence of the double paradox is very obvious. But from Jesus: "For to him who has will be given, and from him who has not will be taken away."

A second and very similar example is the dictum of Jesus that, "Whoever gains (saves) his life loses it; and whoever loses his life gains (saves) it." There are also three sources for this saying in our present texts, one is in Q whence it appears in Matt 10:39 and Luke 17:33, another is in Mark 8:35 which is copied into Matt 16:25 and Luke 9:24, and a third is in John 12:25. In this case, however, there was a version of the original saying in Q and it can still be seen in the sharp double paradox of Luke 17:33: "Whoever seeks to gain his life will lose it, but whoever loses his life will preserve it." Once again, the tradition was not too happy with this dark aphorism. Their changes focus once again on the second half of the parallel saying. Even before Mark an interpretive "for my sake" was inserted in this section and it can still be seen in Matt 10:39; 16:25 and Luke 9:24. But Mark himself made it even more precise and in

8:35 reads: "For whoever would save his life will lose it; and whoever loses his life *for my sake and the gospel's* will save it." John 12:25 is possibly the clearest commentary with this form: "He who loves his life loses it, and he who hates his life *in this world* will keep it *for eternal life*."

I have cited only two examples but once again they are classic cases. A double and parallel paradox involving a twin frustration of common-sense expectation comes from Jesus. The tradition proceeds valiantly to remove the paradox, especially the second and more difficult part, and to translate paradoxical aphorism into the new proverbial wisdom of the Christian challenge.

Beyond Wisdom

The American biblical scholar W. A. Beardslee has already noted some of these aspects of linguistic change between Jesus and the tradition, although in hyperbolic rather than paradoxical texts, and in these cases the tradition is more tolerant of such language.

Two of his main conclusions are of present interest. In comparing different versions of individual proverbs and different layers of the Synoptic and Thomas Gospels, he noted a steady escalation from banal truism to hyperbolic and paradoxical challenge. Even more significantly, he argues that this gradual intensification operates in reverse to the historical sequence of the tradition so that the actual historical development was *from* intensified paradox *to* generalized truism. "The intensification of the Synoptic proverbs is, by its closeness to the function of the parable, to be regarded as a trait of the tradition at a very early stage (indeed, of Jesus himself)." The function of such hyperbolic and paradoxical sayings, which Beardslee derives as I do from the tradition's origins in Jesus, is summed up as follows: "The paradox of intensified antithesis is putting pressure on the very presupposition on which the clusters of wisdom insights had been gathered together. This presupposition is the project of making a continuous whole out of one's existence." Clearly, then, these proverbs were not *intensified*.

73 Form and Parody

They started as paradoxical aphorisms from Jesus and they were muted and *de*intensified by the tradition.

This would be exactly my own contention. Jesus is using paradoxical aphorism or antiproverb to point us beyond proverb and beyond wisdom by reminding us that making it all cohere is simply one of our more intriguing human endeavors and that God is often invoked to buttress the invented coherence. There is nothing wrong with making a whole of one's existence as long as one does it in conscious knowledge that world is our supreme play and that we encounter the Holy in its eschatology.

I recall the terrible anguish of *Canto 116* as the end was already near for Ezra Pound:

> I have brought the great ball of crystal;
> who can lift it?
> Can you enter the great acorn of light?
> But the beauty is not the madness
> Tho' my errors and wrecks lie about me.
> And I am not a demigod,
> I cannot make it cohere.
> If love be not in the house there is nothing—
> The voice of famine unheard.
> How came beauty against this blackness.

It is liberation to realize that coherence is *our* invention, that there is beauty in the blackness, and that beyond coherence lies transcendence. But as Pound had already reminded another poet from out the pain of *The Pisan Cantos*: "So very difficult, Yeats, beauty so difficult." And it is out into that dark and difficult beauty that the paradoxical aphorisms of Jesus would lead us.

5. Beatitude

The form of *beatitude*, best known in Christian tradition from the Sermon on the Mount, can serve as a pivot from the linguistic iconoclasm of Jesus to that of Borges. I am using the term beatitude for the form and including in it both blessings and their corresponding curses.

Proverb to Prayer

The beatitude is a form of language located somewhere between a proverb and a prayer. It is a link between Israel's sapiential and cultic traditions. It declares "blessed" or "happy" the one who acts in a certain way and it is often accompanied by an antithetical parallel declaring the opposite type to be "cursed" or "unhappy."

From a cultic setting there are the opening words of Psalm 1, "Blessed is the man who walks not in the counsel of the wicked, nor stands in the way of sinners, nor sits in the seat of scoffers." Or, again, the opening of Psalm 128, "Blessed is every one who fears the Lord, and walks in his ways." In a sapiential setting there is the list of beatitudes given in Ecclesiasticus (Ben-Sirach) 25:8–10: "Happy is he who lives with an intelligent wife. . . . Happy is he who has gained good sense. . . ." There is a more interesting set in Wisdom 3:13–14 where a greater beatitude is attributed to spiritual virtue than to physical integrity. "Blessed is the barren woman who is undefiled. . . . Blessed also is the eunuch whose hands have done no lawless deed." This last set is challenging the wisdom tradition to exalt virtue over health and to find the greater happiness in the former. But all of this stays safely within standard conventional wisdom.

Blessed the Poor

I shall take only one example from Jesus, the first beatitude given now in both Luke 6:20 and Matt 5:3 in what is usually called in tribute to Matthew's editorial genius, the Sermon on the Mount. Luke 6:20 reads, "Blessed are you poor, for yours is the kingdom of God." As this sentence stands now there is no clear presumption that it means: "Blessed are you poor *on earth,* for yours *will be* the kingdom of God *in heaven.*" Yet once again the tradition moves immediately to explain and to clarify the radicality of Jesus' words. Matt 5:3 inserts into it a qualification: "Blessed are the poor *in spirit*, for theirs is the kingdom of heaven." Surely, Matthew thinks, Jesus could not have meant literally that all and only the physically or financially poor were blessed. This is, of course, exactly what Jesus meant but meant in iconoclastic challenge as also with case parody and paradoxical counterproverb. The solution found in Luke, presumably effected already in Q, is to make a clear qualification of "now" and "will be . . ." in the next two beatitudes in 6:21 and to conclude even more clearly in 6:22 with this future date specified as "reward in heaven." The tradition has changed a radical and iconoclastic antibeatitude whose protasis and apodosis are now on earth into one whose protasis is here on earth but whose apodosis is hereafter in heaven. But what Jesus said was not that. He said, most simply and succinctly: "Blessed the poor, theirs the kingdom."

He did not promise a future God for and after a present pain. He asserted the simultaneous and not the successive presence of poverty and God. I term this form of speech *antibeatitude* because it deliberately opposes and contradicts the formal beatitudes of the tradition. The form is clearly discernible to a modern student of the comic spirit like Wylie Sypher whose work I cited so often in my First Variation. "In the Sermon on the Mount, Jesus tells us with the voice of Innocence that we must accept the ridiculous as the basis of morality: 'Blessed are the meek, for they shall inherit the earth.'"

From an Apocryphal Gospel

In Borges's fifth book of poems, *In Praise of Darkness*, is a prose-poem entitled "From an Apocryphal Gospel." This fragmentary apocryphon consists of a series of terse sayings, numbered from 3 to 51, which take very well-known maxims of Jesus and affirm the opposite. They are, in other words, antibeatitudes. Many of them use the positive form of beatitude starting with "Blessed" (5, 7, 9, 11, 12, 13) or "Happy" (47-51) but the fragment opens with the negative beatitude or curse, "Wretched are the poor in spirit; for what they were on earth, so shall they be in their graves." That is an excellent counter to both Matt 5:3 and Luke 6:20 but it does not touch Jesus' antibeatitude since Jesus placed both poverty and God on this side of the grave. One knows here not hereafter whether Jesus' words are true or false. When Borges says, "Blessed are the pure in heart: for they already see God" he is opposing the futurity of reward in Matt 5:8 but he is in absolute agreement with the simultaneity of Jesus himself in the saying on poverty and the kingdom of God.

The difficulty is that it is not really possible to parody or render paradoxical the language of Jesus. Since it is parodic already, one cannot really attack it from that side except in so far as one can offer better parody or more devastating paradox than that suggested by Jesus and against the same objects. For example, Borges says, "Resist evil: but without either wonder or wrath. Whoever shall smite thee on thy right cheek, turn to him the other also, so long as thou be not moved by fear." (I admit to echoes from Gibran rather than Jesus as I read that sentence.) The saying of Borges is a possible challenge to the version of Matt 5:39 but it is very weak compared to the case parody of Jesus. It seems almost sensible!

In terms of form this means that the antibeatitudes of Jesus are being changed into beatitudes more acceptable to a sapiential and cultic tradition which had already solved the problem of present undeserved suffering in terms of future heavenly reward. But while Borges can successfully pose antibeatitudes to these latter adaptations, he cannot succeed against Jesus, for there antibeatitude is already present and to negate a negation puts one right back in the positive once again.

This is why it seems to me that the most telling parts of the apocryphal gospel invented by Borges are not those places where he parodies language which was originally parodic and iconoclastic with Jesus. This seems true even where his targets are the effects of traditional attempts to render such parodies and antibeatitudes back into sensible ecclesiastical teaching. The parts that strike me most forcibly are sections where he moves directly into paradox for himself: "It is the gate that chooseth, and not the man," or "Nothing is built upon rock: for all is built upon sand: but let each man build as if sand were rock."

But what is important is that just as Jesus played iconoclastically with his own legal, sapiential, and cultic tradition, so is Borges playing now with Jesus' language or at least with the tradition's rendition of it. So that both Jesus and Borges fall under what may be the greatest beatitude of them all. From a letter by the poet Emily Dickinson to Louise and Frances Norcross in early spring of 1881: "Blessed are they that play, for theirs is the kingdom of God."

6. NOVEL

The preceding section pivots the discussion in the rest of this Second Variation primarily to Borges. But one preliminary comparison. The comic eschatology of Jesus involves an iconoclasm on all the major forms of his spiritual tradition. That of Borges focuses the comic subversion on one giant and central aspect of our literary heritage, the tradition of the Book. And especially on its most fascinating example, the Realistic Novel, that beloved child born to Mimesis in the years of its dotage.

Footnotes in Stories

By footnotes I do not mean the perfectly normal notes which accompany many of the essays in a collection such as *Other Inquisitions 1937–1952*. Borges uses references there for the two standard purposes of all such footnotes: either for *factual* material giving, say, biographical or bibliographical specifics and/or for *subsidiary* material of lesser importance than that contained in the body of the text. What interests me at the moment is those footnotes which appear, not in his essays, but in his stories.

Such footnotes are much more numerous in earlier works. The first English translation of his stories was *Ficciones* in 1962 and this contained two Spanish collections from 1941 and 1944. The former collection of eight stories had sixteen footnotes spread over six stories, but the latter one, originally holding six stories, used only two notes and in the same story. In the Afterward to his most recent anthology of stories, *Dr. Brodie's Report*, written in 1970 and translated almost immediately, Borges says, "Since 1953, after a longish interval of composing only poems and short prose pieces, these are the first stories I have written." But this group of eleven stories does not contain a single footnote. Their omission is presumably due to his prefatory confession of having "given up the surprises inherent in a baroque style." Be that as it may, and I have noted earlier how little I think he has really changed, I wish to study these pseudofootnotes under three different aspects: their presence, their content, and their source. It will soon appear that the reason Borges started to omit them was the speed with which he exhausted their possibilities.

First, the *presence* of these notes. We usually make a rather simple distinction between works of fiction, for example, novels and short stories; works of opinion, such as reviews, essays, theses; and works of fact of which genealogies, chronicles, and news reports are obvious examples. Where does one find footnotes in all this? They are seldom present in works of fiction or of fact unless in some creative mixture of these types of writing, but they are the hallmark of works of opinion. In such works their predominant function is to give factual data. When they are no more than asides of opinion they probably should be omitted as textual self-indulgence. You think of footnotes especially, then, as pointing toward fact in works of opinion or criticism. The very presence of footnotes in Borges's stories makes one forget that these stories are about fictional data and not essays, reviews, opinions about factual data. Footnotes, and similar technical devices, led Harss and Dohmann to conclude that, "To give himself freedom of movement, he has invented his own genre, halfway between the essay and the story." And thereby, as we shall see later, he has forced us to explain to ourselves exactly what is the difference between essay and story, or between fact, opinion, and fiction. As Thomas E. Lyon has put it, "The technique of liberally appending both true and untrue footnotes throughout a short story confuses the normal, orderly distance between fiction and fact. The footnote supposedly is fact, in most writing, and should give true pertinent information. Incorporating footnotes into creative prose confuses traditional fictional limitations; Borges has mastered the technique." More succinctly, from Alastair Reid, "He has even succeeded in making scholarship a device of the imagination."

Second, the *content* of such footnotes. I shall use as paradigm a story discussed earlier, the 1940 "Tlön, Uqbar, Orbis Tertius," which, to my knowledge, holds the record with its six footnotes. Three of these notes are what I earlier termed subsidiary since they give us further but less important information. On Tlön, "A century, in accordance with the duodecimal system, signifies a period of one hundred and forty-four years." It must be true (and so then must Tlön) since it's in a footnote. Another one admits the serious problem "of the *matter* of which" the objects from Tlön which are being inserted into our planet will be made. In a third note we find that Tlön holds that, "All men who repeat one line of Shakespeare *are* William Shakespeare." (But Shakespeare, we know, really existed. Therefore.) The other three notes are even more interesting. In "Volume XLVI of *The Anglo-American Cyclopedia*" there was inserted four additional pages on the fictional land of Uqbar complete with bibliography. One work is by "Silas Haslam: *History of the Land Called Uqbar*, 1874" and a footnote informs us that "Haslam has also published *A General History of Labyrinths*." This fictional-factual note is followed a few pages later by one which is real-factual, "Russell (*The Analysis of Mind*, 1921, page 159) conjectures that our planet was created a few moments ago, and provided with a humanity which 'remembers' an illusory past." But Bertrand Russell did write this, therefore, of course, Silas Haslam must also be true. And the final example is on the "millionaire ascetic, Ezra Buckley" who had the distinction of expanding the secret society's plot to invent a fictional land into the creation of a fictional planet. A footnote tells us, fictionally-factually, that "Buckley was a freethinker, a fatalist, and an apologist for slavery."

The main steps are already clear. First, the very presence of footnotes in fictional stories deliberately confuses fiction, opinion, and fact. Second, their content can be purely factual (Russell), a mix of fiction (Tlön) and fact (Shakespeare), or fictional-factual, that is, pseudofactual (Haslam, Buckley). Most of Borges's notes fit into one or other of these three types.

Third, and finally, the *source* of these footnotes. Imagine three levels *in* a story: Author, Narrator, Character (Borges is a prior level *outside* the story). In a typical Borges piece there will be an Author ("I") telling a story involving a manuscript written by a Narrator (possibly also "I") and involving certain Characters. There are actually cases where footnotes have been inserted at each level, by Author, Narrator, and even by Character. By the Author: the six notes in "Tlön" seem to come from the Author. By the Narrator: read "Deutsches Requiem" which has five notes. It is written as the first-person deposition of a captured and condemned Nazi war criminal. This Narrator himself inserts the second footnote but all the others come from the Author whose presence is divulged only through such interjections. The Author, for example, footnotes at one place: "It has been necessary to omit a few lines here." Finally, in one absolutely classic example even a Character gets to insert a footnote. In the 1941 story "The Garden of the Forking Paths," the Author overtly opens the story to introduce the Narrator whose confession to spying and murder then follows in the first person. The deposition of the imprisoned spy (Narrator) mentions that a fellow spy named Viktor Runeberg had been "murdered" by Captain Richard Madden of British counterintelligence (Character). At this point the following footnote appears: "A malicious and outlandish statement. In point of fact, Captain Richard Madden had been attacked by the Prussian spy Hans Rabener, alias Viktor Runeberg, who drew an automatic pistol when Madden appeared with orders for the spy's arrest. Madden, in self defense, had inflicted wounds of which the spy later died.—*Note by the manuscript editor.*" This note, written by one of Madden's superiors, is actually a footnote by a Character or is as close to it as anyone can come. This blurs completely the usual distinctions of Author, Narrator, and Character.

And the point? John Stark has summarized it most accurately in comparing "Tlön" with Vladimir Nabokov's *Pale Fire*. "Their imitation of forms that seem to many people more realistic than fiction convinces the reader that genres are not as distinct as he thought and that the difference between reality and imaginative creation is not clearcut." This is precisely and exactly what is at stake. "Both Nabokov and Borges believe that the imagination is more important and more real in the most significant sense than 'reality.'" Or, even more simply, from Wallace Stevens, "The imagination, the one reality / In this imagined world." So much, then, for parodic or pseudofootnote.

Reviews of Unwritten Books

Pseudofootnotes undermine from within, pseudoreviews from without. We know that there are Authors who write Books and that there are Reviewers who write Reviews and that the latter presume the former. Turn, then, to "The Approach to Al-Mu'tasim" which first appeared in the final pages of Borges's 1936 collection *Historia de la eternidad*. It is also the first of those stories which were eventually to make him internationally famous. It is an essay or review of a book which was never written by an author who never existed.

The opening and closing sections of this pseudoreview consist of pugnacious comments by the Author-Reviewer against *other reviewers* who had previously discussed the book in question. The reviewers in the opening section concerned themselves with the problems of the work's genre: "Both indicate the detective story mechanism of the novel and its mystic undercurrent." Those cited in the closing discussion were interested in the book's sources or precursors. We seem to be quite safely ensconced within an essay or review and since we are told at the start that Dorothy L. Sayers wrote a prologue to the book and at the end that Eliot compared it with *The Faërie Queen*, all things seem to be quite normal. Within these frames of critical dialogue with other reviewers, the Author-Reviewer gives the book's publication history, plot summary, and his own criticism of its contents.

The Reviewer has never been able to find a copy of the original 1932 version entitled "The Approach to Al-Mu'tasim" which he presumes far simpler and superior to the 1934 revision retitled "The Conversation with the Man Called Al-Mu'tasim," and subtitled "A Game with Shifting Mirrors." (This might be considered as a faint warning to the original readers to be careful. It was apparently not enough warning for one of Borges's friends who tried to order the work directly from London after reading Borges's pseudoreview.) The plot concerns a Moslem law student who has killed a Hindu during a riot. Forced to flee, he meets a grave robber who so hates and curses a woman of the robber caste that the fascinated student goes in search of her. This downward journey from hatred to that hatred's object eventually deposits the student among the very dregs of Indian society. Then a similarly caused but reversed and upward journey takes place. Amid all the human degradation he encounters suddenly "some mitigation in this infamy: a tenderness, an exaltation, a silence in one of the abhorrent men." Deciding that this must be the refracted ray of some supreme holiness, he determines to search the world for the man whence any such holiness must emanate. At the end of his "insatiable search" he arrives back in Bombay, near where his downward search had first begun, "at a gallery 'at the rear of which there is a door hung with a cheap and copiously beaded mat curtain; from behind it there emanates a great radiance,'" as the Reviewer quotes from the book under review. The Reviewer continues his summary: "A man's voice—the incredible voice of Al-Mu'tasim—urges him to come in. The student draws back the curtain and steps forward. The novel ends." In his comments the Reviewer prefers the 1932 version where Al-Mu'tasim "is to some degree a symbol" to the 1934 one where "the novel sinks into allegory." In this latter version Al-Mu'tasim is clearly God, and the story is the search of the soul for God. But in the former edition there is the hint that, if he is God, this God "is also in search of

83 Form and Parody

Someone" and so on "to the end—or better, the endlessness—of Time, or on and on in some cyclical form."

This pseudoreview entangles us in at least four different layers of search: Poem, Novel, Review, Story. A terminal footnote refers to the novel's precursor, a mystical Persian *poem* in which the birds search for their king, the Simurg, only to discover at the end "that *they* are the Simurg, and that the Simurg is each one of them and all of them." This first layer gives way to that of the *novel* itself where the same "identity of the Seeker and the Sought" is noted by the Reviewer. (This is cited from lines moved up into the text in *The Aleph* collection but forming the second paragraph of the terminal footnote in the *Ficciones* anthology.) There is a third layer, the search of the *review* for an understanding of the novel itself: is the searcher again the sought? Finally, there is the *story* by Borges we are reading and in which we are searching for what—for ourselves?

Marvin D'Lugo has summarized these layers by saying that, "The critic, the reader and the law student become, to varying degrees, the participant-protagonist of the work." And he has also pointed out what this game with shifting mirrors effects. "In the selection of such literary structures there is more to be found than the mere attempt to achieve a clever parody; the borgian artifice is aimed at a formal 'self-consciousness' in the work, one in which the text functions to revise in the reader the very basis of the latter's perception of reality and fiction."

Projects for Unwritten Books

Pseudoreviews subvert from afterwards; pseudoprojects attack from beforehand. If you can review a book that was never written, why not project one that never will be written? Borges has also written a story about a writer who writes a plot summary instead of the novel itself.

At the start of "Theme of the Traitor and the Hero" the Author records, "I have imagined the following argument, which I shall doubtless develop (and which already justifies me in some way), on profitless afternoons. Details, revisions, adjustments are lacking; there are areas of this history which are not yet revealed to me; today, the third of January of 1944, I dimly perceive it thus: . . ." Reviews, footnotes, projects, all pseudo, and all circle in parody around the realistic novel. The critic Robert Scholes sums up the result by nothing that, "It is hard to see how fiction could insist more resolutely on its fictional character."

Real and Imaginary Authors

Authors can be *real* like Shakespeare, or *imaginary* like "the Bombay lawyer Mir Bahadur Ali" who wrote about Al-Mu'tasim. And real authors can have *real works* (Hamlet) or even *imaginary works* attributed to them. But imaginary authors can receive only imaginary works. When this very simple typology is applied to Borges's stories it is obvious that he has played with every possibility in it.

I have already discussed "Averroes' Search" whose protagonist is a real author introduced to us as he "was writing the eleventh chapter of his work *Tahafut-ul-Tahafut* ("Destruction of Destruction"), in which it is maintained, contrary to the Persian ascetic Ghazali, author of the *Tahafut-ul-falasifa* ("Destruction of Philosophers"), that the divinity knows only the general laws of the universe." I take that to be an imaginary work of Averroes.

But if one can envisage imaginary works of real authors, what could Borges, even Borges, possibly do with real works of real authors? At first he could play "the irresponsible game of a timid man" as he confesses in the second prologue to his 1935 volume *Historia universal de la infamia*. Most of these stories originally appeared in the newspaper *Crítica* as abbreviated revisions from documentary accounts of internationally infamous characters. Or he could conquer that timidity and produce instead "Pierre Menard, Author of the *Quixote*."

This is his second pseudoessay or pseudoreview. It was published in the literary periodical *Sur* for May, 1939, three years after "The Approach to Al-Mu'tasim" had inaugurated this comic antigenre. In this case, however, the Reviewer ("I") is not just dealing with a single work of one author. He is giving us in posthumous review an author's entire work with special emphasis on one specific project. And the author himself appears as a Narrator ("I") since his letters to the Author-Reviewer carefully frame and penetrate the description of his special project.

The story opens in similar tones of *odium academicum* as with "Al-Mu'tasim." Thus: "It is therefore impossible to forgive the omissions and additions perpetrated by Madame Henri Bachelier in a fallacious catalogue . . ." Then follows an itemized list of Pierre Menard's writings from 1899 to 1934 which mixes in real names and real places. These nineteen items are termed "*visible* works left by this novelist." But it is with an unlisted project that the Author is concerned. Menard had worked for about five years "to produce pages which would coincide—word for word and line for line—with those of Miguel de Cervantes." A real author, Cervantes, and a real novel, *Don Quixote*, but then an imaginary author wants "to continue being Pierre Menard and to arrive at *Don Quixote* through the experiences of Pierre Menard." Not to copy it, of course, and not to modernize it either, and not, as too easy, to transpose himself back to the time of Cervantes and see it through his eyes and write it through his pen. At Menard's death he had completed "the ninth and thirty-eighth chapters of part one of *Don Quixote* and a fragment of the twenty-second chapter" and had burned all his rough drafts (footnoted!). "The text of Cervantes and that of Menard are verbally identical, but the second is almost infinitely richer," according to the Author-Reviewer, and he gives us one concrete example. Cervantes wrote about "truth whose mother is history" and so did Menard in exactly the same Spanish phrases. But for Cervantes in the seventeenth century this was "a mere rhetorical eulogy of history," whereas for Menard in the twentieth "the idea is astounding [he] does not define history as an investigation of reality, but as its origin. Historical truth, for him, is not what took place; it is what we think took place." And that is what can be done with a real book from a real author.

We have already seen the Al-Mu'tasim story as an example

of a single imaginary book by an equally imaginary author. There are also two very interesting examples of pseudoreviews on the complete lifework of two other nonauthors. One wrote fiction and the other wrote theology. Therefore. Exactly.

"An Examination of the Work of Herbert Quain" belongs to that first collection of such stories published in 1941. It is another posthumous review of an author's entire corpus of work, beginning with the usual acrimonious comments on other reviews and sprinkled liberally with real names (Agatha Christie, Gertrude Stein), real places (Roscommon), and real things (*Times Literary Supplement*). As with Menard ("he wrote me from Bayonne on December 30th, 1934"), so also Quain ("he wrote me from Longford on March 6, 1939") becomes for a time the Narrator ("I") within the story, in a letter using real places and precise dates. Four of Quain's books are reviewed. In *The God of the Labyrinth* the detective solves the crime but a concluding paragraph stating that, "Everyone thought that the encounter of the two chess players was accidental," sends the reader back for a second reading and the discovery of the *true* solution! Next comes *April March*: "'I lay claim in this novel,' I have heard him say, 'to the essential features of all games: symmetry, arbitrary rules, tedium.'" Only the third part of this novel exists because it was written *backwards*, hence the "feeble pun" of the title: the march of April backwards into March. There are thirteen chapters. "The first reports the ambiguous dialogue of certain strangers on a railroad platform" on a given day. The next three chapters narrate the events of three possible *preceding* evenings. And the next nine chapters offer three alternative preceding evenings for each of those three evenings. The Author-Reviewer gives a diagram but I'll leave it to your visual imagination. *April March* thus consists of nine alternative novels. After its publication "Quain regretted the ternary order and predicted that whoever would imitate him would choose a binary arrangement." The story reads like a magnificent parody on structuralism written before it had become so prevalent as now it is. Quain's novel did backwards what Ts'ui Pên did forwards in his novel *The Garden of the Forking Paths* from the Borges story of that same title: "In all fiction, when a man is faced with alternatives he chooses one at the expense of the others. In the almost unfathomable Ts'ui Pên he chooses—simultaneously—all of them. He thus *creates* various futures, various times which start others that will in their turn branch out and bifurcate in other times."

And that will suffice on Herbert Quain except to note that the Author says his own story "The Circular Ruins" is derived from Quain's *Statements* which contained eight prepackaged plots for incompetent authors to use.

Finally, there is "Three Versions of Judas" which reviews, again posthumously, the entire corpus of an author's work, but this time he is a theologian not a novelist. It appeared in the second anthology of such stories in 1944. The parody on theological argumentation is quite devastating and the footnotes are probably the best of this antigenre. Three versions of Judas. First, in his 1904 book *Kristus och Judas* Nils Runeberg of Lund proposed that human redemption needed a double sacrifice: "The Word had lowered Himself to be mortal; Judas, the disciple of the Word, could lower himself to the role of informer (the worst transgression dishonor abides)." Under attack by "theologians of all the confessions," Runeberg proposes a second version of Judas in this book's revision. He moved from theology to morality. "The ascetic, for the greater glory of God, degrades and mortifies the flesh; Judas did the same with the spirit. He renounced honor, good, peace, the Kingdom of God, as others, less heroically, renounced pleasure." But all of this was only preparation for the final thesis of his 1909 masterpiece *Dem hemlige Fralsaren*. "God became a man completely, a man to the point of infamy, a man to the point of being reprehensible—all the way to the abyss. In order to save us, He could have chosen *any* of the destinies which together weave the uncertain web of history; He could have been Alexander, or Pythagoras, or Rurik, or Jesus; He chose an infamous destiny: He was Judas." His book is disdained by theologians and this only confirms Runeberg that God does not want his terrible secret propagated abroad. "Intoxicated with insomnia and with vertiginous dialectic, Nils Runeberg wandered through the Streets of Malmö, praying aloud that he be given the grace to share Hell with the Redeemer."

Small, Hard, and Bright

There is one very significant aspect of all these parodic forays at and around the long realistic novel or book. Borges's stories are always very short.

The best single collection of representative stories, essays, and parables by Borges is the 1962 anthology appropriately entitled *Labyrinths*. But notice the subtle prejudice which opens the Preface written by André Marrois of the French Academy (my italics): "Jorge Luis Borges is a great writer who has composed *only* little essays or short narratives. *Yet they suffice* for us to call him great. . . ." Who said that great presumed long so that short demanded explanation and apology?

Certainly not Borges. In the 1941 prologue to his first collection, now in *Ficciones*, he mocks those who "go on for five hundred pages developing an idea whose perfect oral exposition is possible in a few minutes! . . . More reasonable, more inept, more indolent, I have preferred to write notes upon imaginary books." Over thirty years later he is defiantly unrepentant. In a Commentary on "The Maker" appended to *The Aleph* he says that, "Ever since 1934, the writing of short prose pieces—fables, parables, brief narratives—has given me a certain mysterious satisfaction. I think of such pages as these as I think of coins—small material objects, hard and bright, tokens of something else." And in conversation with Richard Burgin he was somewhat caustic about Kafka's novels: "I mean, when you've read the first page of *The Trial* you know that he'll never know why he's being judged, why he's being tried. . ."

Something that Ronald Christ said of Borges is true also of Jesus. "It is, paradoxically, because his themes are so expansive and his views so immense that Borges's stories are so short." In both these cases wit is the soul of brevity.

7. MIMESIS

Critics often speak of Borges's stories as metaphysical fantasies. The term is quite acceptable if it be remembered that the entire thrust of Borges is to render that description redundant and tautologous: metaphysics is a very special form of fantasy. This comes from both the *content* of his real essays and, much more importantly, from the very *form* of his pseudoessays and parodic stories.

The Book as Too Much

I have already indicated how Borges saps our trust in the realistic novel by opposing brevity to its length, plot summaries before its nonadvent, posthumous reviews after its noncompletion, and footnotes which confuse author, narrator, and character, not to speak of fiction, opinion, and fact. But this subversion extends beyond the novel to history, philosophy, and all the works of mind. It is our very notion of "realistic" that is under comic attack.

History: Saúl Sosnowski says that, for Borges, "The primary purpose of all his motifs is to provide joy for the 'fiction maker' and the selected group of seers who will recognize a fictitious web in the no less fictitious history recorded by man."

Philosophy: in an excellent article already cited Frances Wyers Weber recalls that, "Borges confessed to the serious omission in his anthology of fantastic literature of the genre's unsuspected and greatest masters—Parmenides, Plato, Duns Scotus, Spinoza, Leibnitz, Kant, Frances [a Francian slip?) Bradley. In his stories Borges does not set everyday reality against a more convincing 'reality' of thought; in fact, he scrupulously blurs the differences between these two levels. But in the pattern of all of them is the implicit opposition between bewitchment or blind faith and ironic comprehension."

But to say that reality-out-there is copied with mimetic fidelity in any book, be it philosophy or theology, be it history or fiction, be it fantasy or science, is to give too much honor to the Book and at the same time to deny it a greater respect which is its final destiny. Too much *and* too little.

The Book as Too Little

The epicenter of Borges's comic eschatology is not located directly on fiction or even on the Book but rather on the presuppositions of reality and of mimesis through which these have been received in Western consciousness. Once these are weakened it becomes impossible to *overestimate* fiction's revelation of the imagination's total creativity in all the realms of word and book. And then "The Library of Babel" shows us that we have said of Book both too much and too little.

The story is from the 1941 collection which includes so many of the early works we have been considering. It opens with these words. "The universe (which others call the Library) is composed of an indefinite, perhaps an infinite, number of hexagonal galleries. . . ." Thereafter we never hear again of the "universe" but only of the Library.

This bibliocosmic Library is an infinite honeycomb composed "of hexagonal galleries, with enormous ventilation shafts in the middle, encircled by very low railings." Five shelves cover floor to ceiling on four sides of each hexagon and the other sides furnish access to the same level and spiral stairs to above and below. Homogeneity of structure in every hexagon and homogeneity of typography in every book as "each shelf contains thirty-two books of a uniform format; each book is made up of four hundred and ten pages; each page, of forty lines; each line, of some eighty black letters." But there is no connection between title and contents.

No two books have similar content so that the Library contains "everything which can be expressed, in all languages." People wander the galleries seeking *their book* or maybe even *The Book* or at least "the Man of the Book" who read this "book which is the cipher and perfect compendium of *all the rest*" and whom many worship as "analogous to a god." Impious people, it is true, mock this hope that in some secret hexagon *The Book* ("may Thy enormous Library be justified") lies still to be discovered and these maintain instead that "absurdities are the norm in the Library and that anything reasonable (even humble and pure coherence) is an almost miraculous exception."

This story equates Book and World so that the former now becomes dominant. Book is not the feeble copy of World but its creator and conserver. John Updike wrote a piece on Borges for *The New Yorker* magazine in 1965 but evaded facing the full challenge of his subject (my italics): "The view of books as, in sum, an *alternate* creation, vast, accessible, highly colored, rich in arcana, possibly sacred . . . Literate man has heaped up a *counterfeit* universe capable of supporting life. Certainly the traditional novel as a transparent imitation of human circumstance has 'a distracted or tired air.' Ironic and blasphemous as Borges's hidden message may seem, the texture and method of his creations, though strictly inimitable, answer to a deep need in contemporary literary art—the need to impress the fact of artifice." But Borges impresses more than the fact of artifice in literary art. He challenges us to admit the inevitability and ubiquity of artifice in all human life, in all our words and in all our books. Dorothy Turner speaks for Borges much more accurately when she says, against Updike, "The library is not an alternate creation; it is creation, and literature, the dream, sustains the universe."

The Mimetic Fallacy

For almost forty years now Borges has been busily preparing the tomb of Mimesis and has inscribed above its marble portal his favorite word as epitaph: *Perhaps*. His comic thrust lunges straight for the Mimetic Fallacy, that great bared jugular of Western literary criticism which those doughty exposers of fallacious criticism, W. K. Wimsatt and M. C. Beardsley, ignored in their attack on the capillaries of the Intentional and Affective Fallacies. But what if language and literature does not discover reality-out-there but instead creates, conserves, destroys, and recreates reality-in-it?

In a structural approach to the literary genre of *The Fantastic*, Tzvetan Todorov has argued that the appeal of this literature depends necessarily on a sustained hesitation between opting for the uncanny or the marvelous in explanation. But the final result is that, "by the hesitation it engenders, the fantastic questions precisely the existence of an irreducible opposition between real and unreal." Put in other words this means that, "the principle we have discovered may be designated as the fragility of the limit between matter and mind." When fantasy is seen like this it directly challenges the Mimetic Fallacy and invites us, at least with Borges, to tilt at windmills and keep our lance unbroken.

Towards the Source

Jesus has taught us the limits of word and the verbal form in the name of Israel's aniconic God. Or, in "The Words of the Lord to John on Patmos," from Rilke,

> Sometimes when they howl that I'm in ire,
> lovingly I fling my trial of fire
> over those possessive sons of earth.
> And I taste some thing of theirs to see
> whether it is fit for me:—
> if it blazes it has worth
> . . . .
> I am not concerned with form,
> and like jagged lightning is my gaze.
> for I am the fiery storm,

Borges has taught us the limits of book and of literary genre in the name of humanity's playful laughter. Or, as Frost saw in that "West-Running Brook,"

> It is this backward motion toward the source,
> Against the stream, that most we see ourselves in,
> The tribute of the current to the source.
> It is from this in nature we are from.
> It is most us.

I understand these as two sides of the same coin, as inseparable as the line of sea and shore, and both are dedicated not to mimetic paradox but to linguistic honesty.

Third Variation:
Parable and Paradox

> I want to make it quite clear that I am not, nor have I ever been, what used to be called a preacher of parables or a fabulist and is now known as a committed writer. I do not aspire to be Aesop.
>
> Jorge Luis Borges

The preceding Variation already indicated the importance of paradox for both Jesus and Borges. Cases, proverbs, and beatitudes for Jesus or footnotes, reviews, and summaries for Borges were all brought into the shadow of paradox. And not because reality-out-there being itself paradoxical demands a mimetic paradox in our language. Rather does paradox confess our awareness that we are making it all up within the supreme game of language. Paradox is language laughing at itself.

1. PARADOX

This Variation considers paradox as the formal principle of the *stories* of Jesus and Borges and argues that such stories can best be termed *parables* since this is a genre of story composed as narrative paradox. Parable is paradox formed into story.

Throughout this section I am very much indebted to a 1960 article by Heinz Politzer on "Franz Kafka and Albert Camus: Parables for Our Time," as well as to his 1962 book on the former parabler. I have actually borrowed the title for this Variation from this excellent study on *Franz Kafka: Parable and Paradox*. And I would put at the head of this discussion his contention that "the human condition may be desperate but it is not unequivocally serious."

Contemporary Parable

In explaining his definition of parable as *paradox formed into story* Heinz Politzer takes for model the 125th aphorism of Nietzsche's *The Joyful Wisdom* from 1882. The tradition gave Nietzsche the Greek philosopher Diogenes following his lantern's light in search of an honest man. But his own parable offers us a madman instead of a philosopher, seeking God not man, declaring God dead not alive, and repeating his indictment on all, including himself, as the murderers of God. "*We have killed him*—you and I." If, then, the seeker after God is himself among the murderers of God, the paradox forces the final gesture of smashing his lantern to the ground. "Must not lanterns be lit in the morning?" Therefore, "He threw his lantern on the ground, and it broke and went out." We need more light now in the darkness after the murder of God. Therefore, increase the darkness. Which Emily Dickenson had said a little earlier: "To Whom the Mornings stand for Nights, / What must the Midnights—be!"

This paradigmatic example furnishes us with the core elements of parable. The first is paradox. The second is story. And the third is their correlation as paradoxical story. This is accomplished by effecting a structural reversal on a traditional or expected story at its deepest levels. Politzer gives two examples, one from Camus and the other from Kafka.

The Plague. "The only general insight Camus' plague conveys to the reader is the realization that there are no general insights to be gained." Politzer's summary finds its concentrated reflection in this comment of Jarrou to Rieux which Camus placed centrally in his novel. "A hundred years ago plague wiped out the entire population of a town in Persia, with one exception. And the sole survivor was precisely the man whose job it was to wash the dead bodies, and who carried on throughout the epidemic." Once again from Politzer: "For Camus . . . the incomprehensible remains incomprehensible, and a paradox takes the place of any rational maxim conveyed by the narration. It is a kind of meta-didactic prose: at the core of the secret a new mystery is hidden." I would underline that adjective, "meta-didactic," and return to it a little later on.

The Trial. We might expect a story structured in a nice, polite binary opposition as follows: The Law gives sentence of death to one convicted of serious crime but gives no death sentence to one innocent of such crime. Kafka furnishes us with a single reversal of this expectation: the Law sentences K. to death and he never knows of what he is accused. This paradox is concentrated once again in a central incident "Before the Law." (I admit to finding both central incidents in both novels much more devastating in their brevity than the full novels which now contain them.) A man seeks entrance to the Law but the doorkeeper continually denies him entrance. He waits and waits and just before his death he asks the doorkeeper why nobody else ever sought entrance to the Law. " 'No one but you could gain admittance through this door, since this door was intended only for you. I am now going to shut it.' " Once again the paradox gives our expectation a reversal. One expects the Doorkeeper to admit those for whom the door was intended and to deny entrance to the unintended ones. But the parable has the Doorkeeper (the Law) deny entrance to the sole intended one. I underline that this is again a single reversal because in very many of Jesus' parables we shall find a double reversal and their artistry consists especially in the economics of this double reversal in a very short story. Politzer summarizes the vision of Kafka in a phrase that every theologian might well remember. "He created symbols which through their paradoxical form expressed the inexpressible without betraying it."

Biblical Parable

Politzer continues his analysis of the modern parable with some comments on its ancient biblical predecessor. And at this point I must disagree most strongly with his conclusions.

Biblical and contemporary parables agree in posing a metaphysical challenge. What, then, is the difference? "The modern parable differs, however, from its model in that it no longer carries a clear-cut message but is built around a paradox." But what if paradox *is* the clear-cut message?

There are, of course, biblical stories with a clear-cut message but there are also biblical stories which are parables in exactly the same sense proposed by Politzer for their contemporary situation, that is, parables as storied paradoxes. It is hardly fair to blame Politzer for finding clear-cut message in the parables of Jesus since, as we shall see again later and as we have already seen for other forms of his language, the tradition went to a lot of trouble adjusting them to have such clear-cut messages before passing them on to us.

I have already indicated the presence of parable in the Hebrew Bible. Ecclesiastes posed his paradoxes to the wisdom tradition and Ruth did the same for the legal tradition. Indeed, in a rather unusual conversion, Ruth started off as an example or exemplary-story (act like this and all will be well) and was later changed into a parable (what if Obed had divorced Ruth "in obedience" to Ezra-Nehemiah intransigence?). But the most magnificent parable in the Hebrew Bible is the book of Jonah which is the precursor for the parables of Jesus and the distant ancestor of the contemporary parabolic genre.

Scholarship once liked to argue how God got whales into the Mediterranean and prophets into whales and each out of the other without serious structural damage to either. The debate is almost as hilarious as the book of Jonah itself and must have surely rejoiced the iconoclastic soul of its author. Jonah is a parabolic lampoon, a parody directed at the very heart of the Bible. It converts into paradox the prophetic traditions themselves. It is, as John Miles so aptly put it, the Bible laughing at itself.

Imagine, first of all, the expected and polarized activity of prophets and pagans against the biblical background. God calls the prophet to mission and obedience is the immediate response. Amos established the pattern and stressed its ineluctable necessity when he said to King Amaziah of Israel, "I am no prophet, nor a prophet's son; but I am a herdsman, and a dresser of sycamore trees, and the Lord took me from following the flock, and the Lord said to me, 'Go, prophesy to my people Israel'" (7:14–15). Amos was not a professional seer but one called as it were against his will or at least his plans and he had to obey. But not so Jonah. This most unusual prophet is ordered by God to go east to Nineveh and he flees instead west to Tarshish "from the presence of the Lord." The prophet disobeys and it takes the famous and comic transportation by God's great fish to deposit him eventually in the right direction (proleptic Suez Canal?). We also know what to expect of pagans and especially of Ninevites. The three short chapters of the book of Nahum combine high poetry and equal hate in announcing the fall of the Assyrian capitol. "Woe to the bloody city, all full of lies and booty—no end to the plunder" (3:1). This gleeful description of the sack of Nineveh concludes triumphantly, "All who hear the news of you clap their hands over you. For upon whom has not come your unceasing evil?" (3:19). Turn now to the book of Jonah. No sooner has this most recalcitrant prophet announced the divine message in Nineveh than this: "And the people of Nineveh believed God; they proclaimed a fast, and put on sackcloth, from the greatest of them to the least of them. The tidings reached the king of Nineveh, and he arose from his throne, removed his robe, and covered himself with sackcloth, and sat in ashes. And he made proclamation and published throughout Nineveh, 'By the decree of the king and his nobles: Let neither man nor beast, herd nor flock, taste anything; let them not feed, or drink water, but let man and beast be covered with sackcloth and let them cry mightily to God" (3:5–8). From king to kine in sackcloth and ashes. Surely the most massive metanoia in all of biblical tradition.

The parable offers a paradoxical double or polar reversal. We expect prophets to obey and pagans, especially Ninevites, to disobey Yahweh, God of Israel. But the story presents us with a most disobedient prophet and with some unbelievably obedient Ninevites. I would emphasize the literary skill which effects a double paradox in this story as distinct from the single paradox of the contemporary parables seen earlier. But what Politzer found in his modern parables and denied to their biblical predecessors is most certainly present in the case of Jonah. The term *parable*, then, should be used technically and specifically, from ancient to contemporary example, for *paradoxes formed into story by effecting single or double reversals of the audience's most profound expectations*. The structure of parable is a deliberate but comic reversal of the expected story. It is not a literal reversal as if Jonah taught that all prophets were bad and all Ninevites were good. It lays bare the relativity of plot, of any plot, and because it is paradoxical it also precludes the possibility of having its own plot taken literally or absolutely. Parable is, to borrow Rilke's phrase, a "ruin that blazingly belies its name."

Myth and Parable

The function of parable can be clarified by comparing it with myth. I am accepting *myth* in the technical sense given to the term in anthropology and folklore and I accept the definition for it proposed by the French structuralist Claude Lévi-Strauss. In his 1955 article on "The Structural Study of Myth" he argued that "the purpose of myth is to provide a logical model capable of overcoming a contradiction." Edmund Leach comments on this definition by saying that, "In every myth system we will find a persistent sequence of binary discriminations as between human / superhuman, mortal / immortal, male / female, legitimate / illegitimate, good / bad . . . followed by a 'mediation' of the paired categories thus distinguished." Categories in binary opposition to each other must be given surrogate representatives whose reconciliation persuades us that the former opposition is mediated. If one cannot mediate love and war, life and death, it may still be possible to get the Goddess of Love and the God of War reconciled with one another. And if all this sounds too abstract and aseptic Pierre Maranda has restated the theory in more interesting language. "Myth . . . is the expression of the dynamic disequilibrium which is the (acknowledged) powerlessness to build adequate homomorphisms between incompatible and hence disturbing facts. It is the expression of the reluctant acknowledgement that the event is mightier than the structure.

But myth is also and more than anything else the hallucinogenic chant in which mankind harmonizes the vagaries of history—the chant hummed for generations in the minds of man and humming itself in the human mind (that innate dream to reduce continuous randomness to a final pattern) as hinted by Plato and Jung or, better, as amplified by Chomsky and Lévi-Strauss."

It is at this point that a most obvious question can be addressed to such a definition of myth. If one accepts the prevalence of binary oppositions as being fundamental to human thinking and if one accepts myth as mediation of binary contradiction, then, *what is the binary opposite of myth itself?* My own answer is that parable is precisely such a binary opposite and that it creates contradiction where before there was reconciliation and mediation. Just as Victor Turner found that *ritual* was bifurcated into rites of order and disorder, elevation and reversal, so must *story* be dichotomized as myth and parable.

All of which W. B. Yeats told us even more clearly quite some time ago in his "Supernatural Songs,"

> Civilisation is hooped together, brought
> Under a rule, under the semblance of peace
> By manifold illusion; but man's life is thought,
> And he, despite his terror, cannot cease
> Ravening through century after century
> Ravening, raging, and uprooting that he may come
> Into the desolation of reality:
> Egypt and Greece, good-bye, and good-bye, Rome!

Over against the harmonious majors of myth we hear the dissonant minors of parable and are thus prepared for Yeats's ultimate challenge: "The last kiss is given to the void."

2. Parable

It is possible to accept the preceding definition of parable, to agree that the genre's trajectory stretches from Jonah to Kafka, and yet to insist that none of this applies to Jesus since his stories are not parables but examples. They are, one might claim, storied models of conduct or storied warnings against misconduct. They would thus not be parables in the strict sense of storied paradox. And the argument could even be clinched, it would seem, by claiming that Borges himself has said as much.

Borges on Jesus

Borges knows the parables of Jesus. In his 1970 story "The Gospel according to Mark" the medical student Baltasar Espinosa is reading from the gospel to the foreman's family at a house where they are isolated by torrential rains. "Remembering his lessons in elocution from his schooldays in Ramos Mejía, Espinosa got to his feet when he came to the parables." (When a new storm starts on top of the preceding floods, the family, who "lacked any religious faith, but there survived in their blood, like faint tracks, the rigid fanaticism of the Calvinist and the superstitions of the pampa Indian," took Espinosa out and crucified him to save the world just as in the story he had read them.) Borges acknowledges the parables of Jesus.

How then explain what happens in his 1951 essay on "Kafka and His Precursors"? He cites six authors, Zeno, Han Yu, Kierkegaard, Browning, Bloy, and Dunsany as precursors of Kafka. By this term he means that "Kafka's idiosyncracy, in greater or less degree, is present in each of these writings, but if Kafka had not written we would not perceive it; that is to say, it would not exist." It is not that these various writers are working in any conscious literary tradition. It is only looking *backwards* from and after Kafka that one can speak of a common Kafkaesque patterning in their works. "The fact is that each writer *creates* his precursors. His work modifies our conception of the past, as it will modify the future." The objection is now clear. Kafka does not create Jesus as a precursor. For Borges, Jesus and Kafka are not on the same generic trajectory. Why this omission?

The answer becomes evident in reading two more essays in the same *Other Inquisitions 1937–1952* collection. The essay on "Nathaniel Hawthorne" is especially important. Borges begins by accepting Hawthorne's story "Wakefield" as a precursor of Kafka: "The debt is mutual; a great writer creates his own precursors. He creates and somehow justifies them." But we can soon guess why Hawthorne was not included among the elect six precursors of Kafka in the essay of that name. "One of Hawthorne's parables which was almost masterly, but not quite, because a preoccupation with ethics mars it, is 'Earth's Holocaust.'" Hawthorne is an exampler not a parabler, and the final verdict is extremely severe. "His solution was to compose moralities and fables; he made or tried to make art a function of the conscience." And again later: "In Hawthorne the genuine vision was always true; what are false, what are ultimately false, are the moralities he added in the last paragraph or the characters he conceived or assembled, in order to represent that vision."

The same indictment is leveled against H. G. Wells. In "The First Wells" he says that, "Those who say that art should not propagate doctrines usually refer to doctrines that are opposed to their own. Naturally this is not my own case; I gratefully profess almost all the doctrines of Wells, but I deplore his inserting them into his narratives." This clarifies the fact that Borges's dislike of Hawthorne's "moralities" or examples is not their content but their intrusive and disruptive presence.

So even though some of Hawthorne is parabolic he cannot be admitted among the precursors of Kafka because he composed moralities or, in my terms, he was an exampler not a parabler. And I presume that this is exactly what Borges thinks of Jesus' stories as well. For Politzer they contained "a clear-cut message" as distinct from a paradox and for Borges, I conclude, they are "moralities and fables." But is all this correct? Is Jesus an exampler or a parabler?

The Good Samaritan

I take as paradigmatic case Jesus' story of "The Good Samaritan." The phrase has become part of the language as a cipher for concerned assistance and we seldom realize that as first uttered it was, like square circle, an oxymoron.

I would ask you to forget everything or anything you know

about the story's present setting or editorial interpretation within the Gospel of Luke. Here is the story, the whole story, and nothing but the story:

A man was going down from Jerusalem to Jericho, and he fell among robbers, who stripped him and beat him, and departed, leaving him half dead. Now by chance a priest was going down that road; and when he saw him he passed by on the other side. So likewise a Levite, when he came to the place and saw him, passed by on the other side. But a Samaritan, as he journeyed, came to where he was; and when he saw him, he had compassion, and went to him and bound up his wounds, pouring on oil and wine; then he set him on his own beast and brought him to an inn, and took care of him. And the next day he took out two denarii and gave them to the innkeeper, saying, "Take care of him; and whatever more you spend, I will repay you when I come back."

A perfectly balanced drama in four acts. In the first act the robbers do three things: strip, beat, and leave for dead. In the second and third acts the Priest and Levite do nothing. But in the fourth act the Samaritan negates the robbers by an opposite three counteractions: medication, transportation, shelter.

How is the story to be interpreted? The tradition's answer is unanimous. Its first evangelical interpreter, Luke, takes it as an example and has Jesus conclude with, "Go and do likewise." And a contemporary philosopher, Paul Ricoeur, concurs, "The parable has turned the story into a pattern for action."

I have asked you to ignore the present gospel setting of the story and I would ask you also, for a moment, to forget you know it comes from Jesus. This is admittedly artificial but it is a necessary discipline in order to see with fresh eyes a story we have never read with sufficient attention. Roland Barthes has said that "the (actual) author of a narrative should not be confused with the teller of the story; the traces of the teller are immanent to the story and therefore perfectly accessible to semiological analysis." I shall be concerned with the *implicit narrator* rather than the historical author (Jesus). And just as there is an implicit narrator in any story so there can also be an *implicit hearer* or audience. As Tzvetan Todorov wrote concerning the implied audience in fantastic tales, "It must be noted that we have in mind no actual reader but the role of the reader implicit in the text (just as the narrator's function is implicit in the text)." For example, who is the implied narrator and implied hearer in a story about a U.S. destroyer and a German submarine during World War II if it is entitled "The Enemy Below" or "The Enemy Above" or "The Enemies"? If, then, we ignore our knowledge that Jesus is the historical author for this story of the Samaritan, what can you learn about its implied narrator and implied audience from within the story itself?

Notice the way in which the actors are introduced into the drama: a man going down from Jerusalem to Jericho, a Priest, a Levite, a Samaritan. I would make two conclusions from this, and they are literary judgments, not absolutes. First, the story is told by a Jewish narrator to a Jewish audience. Places known to Jews (Jerusalem, Jericho) and functions equally well known to them (Priest, Levite) are not explained or specified in any way. Therefore they do not need to be. But the outsider, the Samaritan, is specified exactly in his socioreligious situation. Recall the male chauvinism that gives us Senators and Lady Senators or that describes a woman as "an attractive grandmother" but seldom reciprocates on "a handsome grandfather." And notice the different implications of those two adjectives: handsome in itself but attractive for others/males. An outsider thinks of Jews and Samaritans. A Jew, naturally, thinks of us and Samaritans. Second, the story is most likely told in a Jerusalem setting. The choice of the Jerusalem-Jericho road is made either because it is generally notorious for such robbery ("A man was crossing Central Park late at night . . .") or because it locates narrator and hearers in Jerusalem so that one's first instinct in detailing a journey is to make it from there. If I have to give students a concrete example of a journey it would usually be "from Chicago to . . ." This setting in Jerusalem is also corroborated by the choice of Temple functionaries later in the story.

A Jewish narrator tells a Jerusalem audience a story in which Temple functionaries fail in human kindness and the outcast Samaritan succeeds superbly in helping the wounded Jew. You will note how it is taken completely for granted that this man is a Jew and can be identified obliquely as "a man going down from Jerusalem to Jericho" without any further social or religious qualifications. What would be the reaction of such an audience to such a story. Imagine a contemporary parallel. A Roman Catholic priest preaches as follows from a Belfast pulpit one Sunday. A "man from the Falls Road" lies wounded; a Roman Catholic priest passes by; an IRA member passes by; a Protestant terrorist stops and assists him. How does the congregation react? Does it hear: Help those in need, or, even, love your enemies? Any audience so parabled knows immediately and viscerally that an example story demanding love of enemies *should put the enemy or outsider wounded by the roadside and have him helped by such as are in the audience* and not vice versa. An example puts the Samaritan in trouble and has the Jew help or puts the terrorist in the afflicted position and has the Catholic stop to help. Examples persuade but parables provoke.

The story of Jesus is not an example but a parable. It presents the audience with a paradox involving a double reversal of expectations. The forces of good (Priest, Levite) do evil; the forces of evil (Samaritan) do good. It is exactly the same structure as in Jonah where prophets disobey and Ninevites repent. And it is exactly the same structure found earlier in Jesus' paradoxical counterproverbs: the loser saves, the saver loses; who has receives, who has not loses. But just as with Jesus' case parodies, counterproverbs, and antibeatitudes, so now with his parables, the tradition has attempted to divert their radical thrust back into more normal channels so that parables become examples.

I said earlier that the tradition had been unanimous in taking "The Good Samaritan" as an example rather than as a parable. If you turn, however, from direct commentary by exegetes to indirect commentary by novelists the tradition is not quite so unanimous. Leo Tolstoy, as might be expected, reflects an example interpretation in his story "What Men Live By." Simon the shoemaker sees something near a roadside shrine. "To his surprise it really was a man, alive or dead, sitting naked, leaning motionless against the shrine. Terror seized the shoemaker, and he thought, 'Some one has killed him, stripped him, and left him here. If I meddle I shall surely get into trouble.'" But he relents, covers the man with his own coat and takes him home. He helps Simon so adeptly at his craft that "from all the district round people came to Simon for their boots, and he began to be well off." Finally, the stranger reveals that he is an angel but before he departs he recalls their first meeting, "When the man saw me he frowned and became still more terrible, and passed me by on the other side. I despaired; but suddenly I heard him coming back."

Henry Fielding, however, offers a far different retelling of the story. Since he is much more interested in parodic satire than in exemplaric conduct he senses far more accurately than Tolstoy the parabolic nature of the story of Jesus. The incident is in chapter 12 ("*Containing many surprising Adventures, which* Joseph Andrews *met with on the Road, scarce credible to those who have never travelled in a Stage-Coach*") of his novel *Joseph Andrews*.

Joseph is traveling on foot as was the man in Jesus' story and exactly the same fate befalls him. "He was met by two Fellows in a narrow Lane, and ordered to stand and deliver . . . and both together fell to be-labouring poor *Joseph* with their Sticks, till they were convinced they had put an end to his miserable Being: They then stript him entirely naked, threw him into a Ditch, and departed with their Booty." It is an eighteenth century version of Jesus' summary, "fell among robbers, who stripped him and beat him, and departed, leaving him half dead."

The *successive* arrival of Priest, Levite, and Samaritan is developed by Fielding into the arrival of a coach so that there is a *simultaneous* dialogue between the negative and positive reactions of the travelers to the man in the ditch. The coach has six main characters: Postillion, Coachman, Lady, her Footman, Old Gentleman, Young Lawyer. These engage in parodic debate over four major points (recall the Samaritan's action): to stop or not, to help or not, to transport or not, to clothe or not.

To Stop or Not? The Postillion wants to stop. The Coachman objects that "we are confounded late, and have no time to look after dead Men." The Lady wants to stop but out of curiosity.

To Help or Not? The Postillion alights and reports about Joseph. The Lady wants to drive on (naked!) and the Old Gentleman concurs (robbed!), but the Lawyer warns them that they might be legally responsible and that it was "adviseable to save the poor Creature's life, for their own sakes, if possible."

To transport or Not? The Coachman asks who will "pay a Shilling for his Carriage the four Miles" and the two gentlemen refuse to do so. But the Lawyer's reiterated warnings of their legal responsibilities make them all agree "to join with the Company in giving a Mug of Beer for his Fare."

To Clothe or Not? Lawyer and Gentleman refuse because they are cold and wish to keep their overcoats. The Coachman ("who had two great Coats spread under him") and the Lady's Footman refuse lest their coats become bloody. Finally, it is the Postillion who acts: "It is more than probable, poor *Joseph* . . . must have perished, unless the Postillion, (a Lad who hath been since transported for robbing a Hen-roost) had voluntarily stript off a great Coat, his only Garment, at the same time swearing a great Oath, (for which he was rebuked by the Passengers) 'that he would rather ride in his Shirt all his Life, than suffer a Fellow-Creature to lie in so miserable a Condition.'"

Coachman, Lady and Footman, Lawyer and Gentleman all refuse assistance or do so for self-serving reasons. But it is the Postillion, the lowest member of the Coach hierarchy, one whose rebuked swearing is an omen of his future penal exile, who *stops*, who *goes* to Joseph, and alone will *clothe* him with his own and only outer garment and so make transportation to shelter possible.

It is clear that Fielding presumes one should give aid to those in distress and that Jesus extends such aid even to enemies. But these are the *presuppositions* rather than the *points* of their respective stories. To say that Jesus or Fielding created their stories to furnish models of neighborliness is to interpret Kafka's *The Trial* is an argument against police brutality and Camus's *The Plague* as a model of medical assistance. I submit, in conclusion, that Fielding has given us the only adequate commentary ever written on Jesus' famous story.

The next step is to see if this generic change effected on "The Good Samaritan" has happened to many more (or all) of Jesus' stories. Were they all originally parables, that is, paradoxes formed into story? Was it the tradition which turned them into examples so that even Borges, seeing exactly what the tradition wanted him to see, ignores Jesus as a parabler, judging that Jesus, like Hawthorne, "tried to make art a function of the conscience"?

Metonymy and Metaphor

For the moment I wish to concentrate on a number of Jesus' parables whose structure is extremely similar to that of "The Good Samaritan" and I shall argue that the tradition has consistently asked us to read them as examples, as stories of how one should or should not act and how God approves or disapproves such action. But first I need to introduce a distinction between metonymy and metaphor.

Roman Jakobson has insisted for over fifty years on the fundamental importance of the difference between "the metaphoric and metonymic poles" in language. In a fascinating article on "Two Aspects of Language and Two Types of Aphasic Disturbances" he proposed this theory: "Every form of aphasic disturbance consists in some impairment, more or less severe, either of the faculty for selection and substitution or for combination and contexture. . . . The relation of similarity is suppressed in the former, the relation of contiguity in the latter form of aphasia. Metaphor is alien to the similarity disorder, and metonymy to the contiguity disorder." He exemplifies the two poles by the psychological test in which a child is asked for an immediate verbal response to the word *hut*. Some children offer the metaphors *den* or *burrow* while others respond with metonyms such as *thatch* (thatch is part of hut) or *poverty* (hut is part of poverty). Jakobson applies his metonymy and metaphor distinction not only to the minutiae of aphasic pathology but on a much wider level because "it is generally realized that romanticism is closely linked with metaphor, whereas the equally intimate ties of realism with metonymy usually remain unnoticed." If language is imagined as a giant grid, one could say that metaphor makes connections along the vertical axes of similarity while metonymy forges contacts along the horizontal axes of contiguity.

The distinction can now be applied to Jesus' parables. The paradoxicality of linguistic world can be shown either in metaphoric or metonymic parables. Metonymic parables will take real or representative *parts-of-world* in order to reduce that world to paradox. Metaphoric parables will do the same but with *miniworlds* or model and miniature worlds. For example, to protest American involvement in the Vietnam War in the sixties some burned draft cards in metonymic protest while others burned the American flag as a metaphoric parable in action. The book of Jonah is metonymic rather than metaphoric because "a prophet" and "the Ninevites" are polar representative *parts* of the biblical world. They are the whole by metonymy and in subverting them the whole is attacked.

"The Good Samaritan" is likewise metonymic and in exactly the same way. Especially in a Jerusalem setting, Priest and Levite, on the one hand, and Samaritan, on the other, are metonyms for a social and religious world in its positive and negative totality.

There are two other metonymic parables of Jesus very similar to "The Good Samaritan." A first one is "The Pharisee and the Publican" in which both go up to the Temple and pray but the prayer of the Pharisee is rejected by God while that of Publican is accepted. Once again, however, much of the paradox is lost on the modern reader who has been indoctrinated by Christian polemics into thinking Pharisees hypocrites and Publicans basically very nice people. An accurate idea of its original impact may be had by stating the following story from a Roman Catholic pulpit some Sunday morning: "A Pope and a pimp went into St. Peter's to pray." No matter where the story goes after such an opening the narrator has placed himself in jeopardy by the initial juxtaposition. So with Jesus' original. Pharisees were the rightly revered moral guides of their times and Publicans were lower level toll collectors considered as constitutionally and professionally dishonest. (Rather like the term politician at the moment.) Jesus' story was a shocking, radical, and double reversal of the metonymic poles of his contemporary ethical world.

A second metonymic parable is that of "The Rich Man and Lazarus" and once again some background is necessary to sense the original shock of Jesus' story. First, very many of Jesus' hearers would presume that health and wealth was an index of divine approval and that poverty and disease was an indication of punishment for sin. Recall that marvelous question in John 9:1. "As he passed by, he saw a man blind from his birth. And his disciples asked him, 'Rabbi, who sinned, this man or his parents, that he was born blind?'" Second, the German exegete Joachim Jeremias has reminded us that a very similar story is known in Egyptian folkore concerning "the journey of Si-Osiris, the son of Setme Chamoïs to the underworld, which concludes with the words: 'He who has been good on earth, will be blessed in the kingdom of the dead, and he who has been evil on earth, will suffer in the kingdom of the dead.' Alexandrian Jews brought this story to Palestine, where it became very popular as the story of the poor scholar and the rich publican Bar Ma'jan." What is interesting about these precursors of Jesus' story is their clear and explicit morality. In the Egyptian version earthly virtue or vice begets future reward or punishment beyond the grave. In the Palestinian variation the unattended funeral of the poor scholar leads to heavenly bliss while the magnificent burial of the rich publican deposits him in eternal thirst. But once again the morality is clear: poor but virtuous is better than rich but dishonest. Third, the section at the end of Jesus' story in Luke 16:27–31 is not part of the original story. The theme of resurrection ("If they do not hear Moses and the prophets, neither will they be convinced if some one should rise from the dead") was a later addition to the narrative. Once again the tradition had difficulty in understanding the story's point and added in the discussion on resurrection to make it more applicable to the post-Easter situation of the community. A similar but more radical change occurs in John 11 where Lazarus, in a different narrative setting, comes back himself from the dead and still the authorities do not believe (12:9–11).

In its original simplicity Jesus' story tells of a rich man whose happy life ends in Hades and of a poor diseased beggar who ended up in the bosom of Abraham. It is *never* said that the beggar is virtuous (like the poor scholar) or that the rich man was dishonest (like the publican Bar Ma'jan) but simply that their earthly roles were reversed in the next life. "But Abraham said, 'Son, remember that you in your lifetime received your good things, and Lazarus in like manner evil things; but now he is comforted, and you are in anguish.'" This is very, very shocking. No sanctions for good and evil but a simple reversal of earthly fortune takes place in the heaven/hell of Jesus' story. Once again a double and polar reversal occurs taking as metonyms for society's economic world the Rich Man and Lazarus who are the protagonists of the story.

These three metonymic parables, subverting social, ethical, and economic world by placing their representatives in acute paradox, have one obvious strength and one equal weakness. What they gain in immediate bite within their original situation is lost for the later reader who has to have so many terms explained before understanding is possible. By the time one knows the significance of Priest, Levite, Samaritan, Pharisee, Publican, Rich Man, Lazarus, the parables are ruined, just like jokes which have to be explained. There are, however, three other parables with very similar structure which are metaphoric rather than metonymic and which have therefore the opposite strength and its corresponding weakness. These may have failed a little in original historical acerbity but they gain thereby a wider and more universal appeal.

The most famous of these metaphoric parables involving a paradoxical double reversal of our expectations is "The Prodigal Son." We expect fathers to offer celebratory banquets to dutiful sons and none to prodigal sons. We expect prodigals outside and dutifuls inside such feasts. But here is a very beautiful story in which we see a prodigal inside feasting and a dutiful outside pouting, and the storyteller is scrupulously fair to father and sons. Yes, it could happen like this and we do not or should not really blame anyone. It was not originally, as Luke now makes it, an example of how not to act in the face of divine mercy but a parable inviting our imagination to a polar reversal of expectation. But notice that the miniworld of father and sons, host and invited/noninvited guests, is a metaphor rather than a metonym for the world at large. Obviously, then, our present title for this story is itself an emphasis and an explanation. A neutral title might be, for example, "The Father with Two Sons."

So also with the parable of "The Great Supper." The original version can be reconstructed from a careful comparison of the various versions still extant in our texts. Of these the version in *The Gospel of Thomas* discovered at Nag Hammadi in Upper Egypt around 1945 is closest to the original story of Jesus. A man decides on a feast and sends out his servant to invite chosen guests while he goes about the preparations. But because of the suddenness of the invitation all must refuse (there were originally a folkloric "three" guests) and by the time the single servant has visited them all and reported back to the host, the master finds himself with a full table and an empty guest list. Angry, probably as much with himself as with his friends, he sends out the servant to bring in whomsoever he can find from the streets outside. Thomas (negative example), Luke (positive example), and Matthew (allegory of the history of salvation) worked valiantly on this story to change it from parable to example, but one can hardly credit the latter two with much success. The story of Jesus was a metaphoric parable with the microcosm of host and guests portraying how our expectation that a host furnish a banquet for friends and not for strangers might be paradoxically reversed so that strangers are present and friends all absent.

One final example, the parable of "The Places at Table": Jesus' story asks us to imagine a perfectly reasonable possibility. A guest grabs the first place at a banquet. Others arrive and the table fills up. Then a guest of special importance arrives and the embarrassed first arrival must cede place and go to the foot of the table. On the other hand, it is also imaginable that an honored guest go to the lowest place and be called up to the seat of honor. These things happen, do they not, the story asks us. Luke's most unhappy interpretation seeks to turn parable into example by introducing a "so that" into the second half of the story: Sit in the lowest place *so that* you will be called up higher and honored before all the guests. It took Borges only two seconds to skewer that piece of false humility in his "From an Apocryphal Gospel." his comment: "It availeth not to be the last so as to be the first." The truth is that parables make notoriously bad examples.

There is probably something profoundly human in the attitude of the tradition to Jesus' parabolic stories. When I read Kafka's parable "Before the Law" to my freshman class at DePaul University most take it as an example and react with either the John Wayne syndrome ("he should have forced his way in"), or the militant activist response ("the doorkeeper should be removed immediately"), or the counterculture attitude ("why didn't he just split?"). Or I am assured that the story is an allegory indicating that one cannot enter heaven until after one's death. It is very difficult and terribly uncomfortable to look straight and unflinching into the heart of parable as parable.

Borges as Parabler

Borges, on the other hand, is clearly a parabler and not a teller of examples, moralities, or fables.

He himself has repeatedly insisted on this point but has also confused the issue by using parable and fable as synonymous as, for example, in the epigraph to this present Variation. There the proposition is that Aesop is a preacher and that fables are parables. He also admits in that Preface to his 1970 collection *Dr. Brodie's Report* that he has never himself used art to preach "except once when I was buoyed up in exultation over the Six-Day War." This refers to the poem "Israel" first published in *Davar* for Fall, 1967.

(An aside on this poem. Borges's most recent volume of poetry *In Praise of Darkness* precedes this poem with another one "To Israel" first published by *Davar* in Spring, 1967. Between these two poems came the Six-Day War of June, 1967. The former work concludes:

> You are in that book, which in its hard
> and complex crystal is the mirror
> of every face that bends over it
> and of God's own face, terribly glimpsed.
> Hail, Israel, defender of God's
> ramparts, in the passion of your war.

And the latter poem finishes like this,

> a man who endures and is deathless
> and who now has returned to his battle,
> to the violent light of victory,
> handsome as a lion in the twelve o'clock sun.

It would seem that political exultation was successfully translated into poetry because the Six-Day War was seen as part of a longer and larger war and because the "political" poem was but a chapter in or continuation of the earlier ode to Israel.)

To return to the original point: Borges reiterated it again about a year after the writing of that Preface when he was visiting the Washington Square campus of New York University. "I don't think I have any moral purpose when I write. When I write, I'm trying to set down some kind of tale, not some kind of fable, but if the reader wants to read something moral into the text, that's all to the good. When I'm writing a story, I'm not thinking in terms, let's say, of political or ethical opinions: I'm merely trying to be true, let's say, to the plot, to the dream, perhaps." Borges is not a fabler, a moralizer, an Aesop. That was clear even without his assurances. But the best term for his stories is parables and the best generic term for their author is parabler. Fables use animals and examples use humans to give a clear-cut didactic message on how or how not to act: Go and do or don't do like this. But parables are what Politzer so aptly called "meta-didactic stories," paradoxes forcing us out into that silent darkness where ethics, like all human creativity, is forged in risk and danger, in fear and trembling.

The terms parable and paradox reoccur again and again in critical studies of Borges. But as in so many other areas concerning him the unpublished doctoral dissertation of James E. Irby from the University of Michigan in 1962 is here most helpful. Paradox is almost the controlling term of his analysis. It appears at the very start with the statement that, "Borges's stories are the varied accounts or dramatizations of the conflicting consequences of this essential confrontation of opposites, which persists as an insoluble paradox. . . . All his themes and motifs exist as polar dualities, simultaneously as hopeful aspiration and as negative limitation or failure. . . . For Borges there is no system of thought or belief . . . which does not contain within itself its own refutation." And again, in summing up his conclusions at the end of the thesis, Irby argues that, "The essence of Borges's thought and artistic method is the paradox, whose tension and clash of opposites is found in all aspects of his narrative work. All elements are defined in terms of their contraries and are joined with them in such a way that their inextricable unity and their sharp differences are simultaneously felt." And do these stories have messages? Irby protects himself behind quotation marks: "Borges's tales are in the manner of parables or legends, whose fundamental 'messages,' however, upset conventional, predictable ideas and force the reader to think and see afresh." To think and see what? I would answer language and the worlds created only in and by language. And I would insist that it is a message to say that there is no total message and it is also a message to insist that such is not cause for alarm.

A final example. Ben Belitt contributed "The enigmatic predicament: some parables of Kafka and Borges" to the 1972 issue of *TriQuarterly* dedicated as *Prose for Borges*. I would disagree very strongly with his confusion of parable and code in his statement that, "The parable, then, is a hermetic directive to the 'elect' through which action is turned into fable." It is an understandable confusion following two thousand years of Christian tradition based on Mark 4 where Jesus' parables are interpreted as codes, impervious to outsiders but easily explicable to insiders.

Elsewhere in his article, however, he suggests a far more satisfying definition of parable, one which specifies what parables as narrative paradoxes can functionally effect. "Finally, as insights, parables serve what might be called an epistemology of *loss*. Their value, as knowledge, is to enhance our 'consciousness of ignorance'—but that is the beginning of wisdom. The vocation of Socrates began with a visit to the Oracle at Delphi and a 'parable,' and ended with a philosopher's conviction that 'I know that I do not know.'"

3. ALLEGORY

This section is a review and a revision of what I said concerning allegory in my book *In Parables*. The need for rethinking that analysis arises both negatively in a growing dissatisfaction with the distinctions there accepted and positively in an attempt to consider allegory under the rubric of play. There is also a quite deliberate shift from a romanticist to a structuralist position.

The major substantive change is that *parable* is no longer opposed to *allegory* but rather to *example* and, then, just as there can be *allegorical examples* so also can there be *allegorical parables*. But in these latter stories, as distinct from the former ones, the paradox at the heart of the narrative must reappear at every level of allegorical reading or interpretation.

Ideas or Images

In Parables argued a distinction between metaphor, in which images led to ideas, and allegory, in which ideas preceded and begot images. The distinction also proposed the ascendancy of image over idea and, therefore, of metaphor over allegory. This seemed a fairly clear differentiation and one for which there was an extremely illustrious pedigree since I could cite Goethe and Coleridge, Yeats and Eliot in its favor.

Since that time, however, I have found it more and more

difficult to answer three questions which cumulatively seem to destroy those distinctions as far as either coherent theory or practical application are concerned. First, what exactly is the difference between an image and an idea? For instance, Borges opened "The Fearful Sphere of Pascal" by saying that, "It may be that universal history is the history of a handful of metaphors," and he closed it with the same sentence. If history is metaphors, images, are even the most abstract philosophies controlled by ideas or by images and what is the difference between them at such a depth? Second, *if* we can so distinguish, how do we know whether a given author moved in creativity from idea to image or from image to idea? For example, in "The Antique Ring" Nathaniel Hawthorne has Edward Caryl tell Clara Pemberton, "You know that I can never separate the idea from the symbol in which it manifests itself." Unless we could declare by critical fiat that a bad story is created from idea to image and all great ones move in the opposite direction, it would seem that a dualism based on such a distinction is of little practical value. Third, *even if* the distinction be accepted *and if* the creative dualism be acknowledged, why should we conclude that the movement from image to idea is intrinsically superior to its opposite? The usual argument is to take bad allegory and explain its failure because of idea's distortion of image and to applaud great allegory (as symbol or metaphor) because of the triumph of image. But, once again, we are back in critical fiat. There might also be other reasons and even more basic ones why some allegories are admittedly bad while others are creatively magnificent.

Robert Scholes and Robert Kellogg have made very precise criticism of this distinction between symbol/metaphor and allegory in their book on *The Nature of Narrative*. The distinction is fundamentally a product of Romanticism where "this invidious distinction sees symbolism as being organic, nonintellectual, pointing to some mystical connection between the mind of the poet and that unreal world which is the shaping mind or soul behind actuality, wearing what we call the 'real' world as its vestment. In this essentially romantic view allegory is contrasted with symbolism as being overtly intellectual and excessively didactic, reflecting the real world in a mechanical and superficial way." And whatever the value of "this invidious distinction" for *lyric poetry*, it is of little value or validity for *narrative art* which "requires an irreducible minimum of rationality which inevitably tames and limits the meaning of the vaguest of images."

If, then, we leave aside this romanticist distinction between image and idea or symbol/metaphor and allegory, what can be said of allegory for now? In this restatement I am very conscious of the accusation of Paul de Man in "The Rhetoric of Temporality" who "tried to show that the term 'symbol' [metaphor] had in fact been substituted for that of 'alleogry' in an act of ontological bad faith" within romanticist criticism.

Borges on Allegory

I indicated earlier the rather harsh strictures of Borges against moral didacticism in Hawthorne even though appended almost as a postscript to many of Hawthorne's stories. Borges is also quite negative on allegory but here he moves far more cautiously than with fables, examples, or moralities.

Borges's most direct discussions of allegory are contained in two essays of 1949. One is "Nathaniel Hawthorne" discussed earlier for his criticism of examples. The other is "From Allegories to Novels" and here the emphasis is exclusively on allegories. He admits immediately our modern prejudice against allegory. "For all of us, the allegory is an aesthetic error." In support of this he quotes Benedetto Croce whose condemnation rests basically on the same distinctions invoked by Goethe, Coleridge, Yeats, and Eliot, and cited by *In Parables*. The symbol derives organically and immediately from artistic intuition but the allegory is generated by an abstract concept. Against Croce Borges cites G. K. Chesterton who argues in favor of allegory. Beatrice, he maintains, is not a *symbol* for the *concept* of faith. The woman and the word are *both* signs for the same virtue and the woman-sign is far richer than the word-sign. Borges concludes, "I am not certain which of the eminent contradictors is right. I know that at one time the allegorical art was considered quite charming . . . and is now intolerable. We feel that, besides being intolerable, it is stupid and frivolous." This repeats what he had said in "Nathaniel Hawthorne." There too he refused to decide. "I don't know whether Chesterton's thesis is valid: I do know that the less an allegory can be reduced to a plan, to a cold set of abstractions, the better it is. One writer thinks in images . . . and another writer thinks in abstractions. . . . A priori, the former are just as estimable as the latter."

In an interview with Robert Lima about ten years later Borges returned to the problem. "I suspect there are two ways of thinking: the logical way, in which we proceed through premises, reasoning, and conclusions, and the nonvigilant way, that of dreams, which is the route not of logical man but of the child or primitive man, in which we think through images, metaphors, or parables. . . . I suppose that the function of literature is to serve as a sort of dream for Man, perhaps helping him thereby to live in reality." This is back to the distinction of idea and image but, instead of exalting one over the other, it says more simply that one can think either in ideas or in images. This was Chesterton's point since he defended allegory as thinking in images and symbols rather than in words and concepts. One might still ask, of course, if it is humanly possible to have idea without image or word without symbol, and what is the difference between these options in any case.

Finally, there are the comments written by Borges as the Foreword for two critical studies of his work. The resemblance between the two introductions makes one wonder if Borges has a set format for all such requests and merely changes author and title for each individual case. In 1964 he thanked Ana María Barrenechea for unearthing "many secret links and affinities" in his work since these proved that "my best writings are of things that were striving to come to life through me, or in spite of me, and not simply allegories where the thought comes before the sign." Allegory is again defined as idea, the thought, preceding image, the sign. In 1968 Borges thanked Ronald Christ for revealing "many secret links and affinities," but this time he went on to affirm that, "I am neither a thinker nor a moralist, but simply a man of letters who turns his own perplexities and that respected system of perplexities we call philosophy into the forms of literature."

What conclusion can be drawn from all this? First, Borges discusses allegory primary within the romanticist negativity which condemns it as idea begetting image, as thought producing sign, as message inventing metaphor. Second, he is not nearly as secure in his criticism of allegory as he is against example stories. Maybe, after all, Chesterton is right and allegory is simply thinking in images rather than controlling images by prior ideas. Carter Wheelock probably summed it up most accurately by saying that Borges "does not mind being called an allegorist if only the implication of didacticism is removed. Stripped of its moralism, allegory becomes a valid and powerful esthetic device, a long metaphor rich in suggestion."

But none of this has really moved the discussion beyond the romanticist esthetic and my objective is to attempt this development before any consideration of allegory in the stories of Jesus.

Motives for Allegory

Why would anyone want to tell a story which can be read on different levels and with diverse meanings? Critics have indicated four major reasons or motives for allegory or, better, four main functional effects of the mode. Allegory circumvents opposition, creates separation, establishes continuation, and reveals structuration. No doubt these four merge and intertwine with one another in any given allegorical work but their distinction is helpful both to note emphases and because they indicate a more and more profound effect of allegory as one moves from the first to the last result.

Opposition. You wish to tell your story, be it to recall the past, to support the present, or to invoke the future, but you must do so in coded fashion because of persecution. The motive here is protection of oneself against oppression and of one's message against censorship. The story communicates to insiders but not to outsiders. This is the motive stressed in Angus Fletcher's book *Allegory: The Making of a Symbolic*

Mode. He says, for example, "allegory . . . appears to express conflict between rival authorities, as in time of political oppression we may get 'Aesop-language' to avoid censorship of dissident thought. At the heart of any allegory will be found this conflict of authorities." And again, later, "Allegory presumably thrives on political censorship." This motive is well known from certain books of the Bible such as Daniel and Revelation and from the apocalyptic tradition in general. Jews persecuted by Syria or Christians oppressed by Rome announced defiantly but allegorically their security in God's ultimate and proximate justice for them and against their imperial persecutors.

Separation. This is the motive for allegory studied by Michael Murrin in *The Veil of Allegory.* For him the primary reason for allegory is less fear of persecution than fear of profanation by misunderstanding. Allegory, he claims, wishes to make a separation within its hearers to divide those who really understand from those who hear but do not comprehend. The story creates deliberately a separation of insiders and outsiders. For example, "the allegorical poet . . . expends much of his energy in protecting his truth from the multitude rather than in communicating it." Fletcher had emphasized the motive of protection against opposition as in the apocalyptic tradition of the Bible. Murrin, on the contrary, stresses the divisive judgment of the prophetic tradition. "The allegorical poet affects his audience more in the manner of a Hebrew prophet than in that of a classical orator." Both speak and cause division, only the few understand while most cannot comprehend the message. The allegorical poet deliberately creates such a minority and rejoices in its elitism, but the prophet does not will it nor rejoice in its presence. He simply mourns its inevitability. I find this interpretation much more persuasive for the allegorical poet than for the Hebrew prophet and would tend to bracket completely everything concerning this latter tradition in Murrin. But allegory can certainly be used in a conviction that only a few will take one's message whole and complete while most will distort and misunderstand it. "He had, therefore, simultaneously to reveal and not to reveal his truth, and for this double purpose he cloaked his truth in the veils of allegory. The many reacted with pleasure to his symbolic tales, and the few knew how to interpret them." This may be acceptable as a motive for allegory but it is somewhat strange as a comment on Hebrew prophecy. There the audience knew all too well what the prophet was saying. The problem was not misunderstanding but disobedience and the result was martyrdom not mystery. Amos's succinct greeting, "Hear this word, you cows of Bashan," was presumably quite clear to the women of Samaria and while one might consider it as veiled allegory it is doubtful if anyone in Israel needed much translation for it.

Continuation. This is a more interesting purpose which intends to strengthen the persuasive power of one's story by basing it on another one which is either better known or more secure in its structure and conclusion. It establishes the continuity of the tradition and makes novelty more acceptable as well as the past more continually viable. When, for example, human actions or historical events are told in terms of the world of nature they take on a borrowed inevitability and an intensely persuasive teleology. If heaven is harvest then of course heaven will come. Edwin Honig noted this motive in his *Dark Conceit: The Making of Allegory.* The new and unproven story corroborates itself by retelling an old and accepted one, and continuation is thereby established and demonstrated. "We find the allegorical quality in a twice-told tale written in rhetorical, or figurative, language and expressing a vital belief. . . . The twice-told aspect of the tale indicates that some venerated or proverbial antecedent (old) story has become a pattern for another (the new) story." Such an antecedent could be nature, the animal world, legend, sacred book, or whatever is judged to strengthen and corroborate the new by establishing continuity with the old.

Structuration. This fourth effect may well be the least obvious but also the most important result of allegory. When a story can be read on many different levels such integrated structuration can be seen as the deliberate traces of divine intentionality. These layered correspondences are there to be found by us because a divine wisdom created all of them, and in finding them we are but climbing similar rungs towards their common source. Allegory reveals at every level of world a similar structuration and this is, as it were, an indirect, and therefore much more powerful argument from design for the existence of God. As early as the fifth century John Cassian taught that there were four separate levels of meaning in the Bible since, for example, *Jerusalem* could mean an historical city in Palestine, Christ and his Church, the human soul, or Heaven. Biblical stories could thus be read in terms of the past of Old Testament promise and New Testament fulfillment, the present of moral action, and the future of eschatological sanctions. If you have any doubt about the power of such a hermeneutic you may recall that it was still viable in the Renaissance which believed, in the words of Meyer Abrams, that "the divine Architect has designed the universe analogically, relating the physical, moral, and spiritual realms by an elaborate system of correspondences."

Against such a background it is clear why allegory and morality became so closely identified. The structures of Old and New Testament, of history and eschatology, of Christ and Church all pressed as models upon the individual human soul which had to do this and avoid that under pain of alienation from all the structures of reality. It was presumably considerations such as these that led to an absolute dismissal of the mode on the part of Henry James. "Allegory to my sense is quite one of the lighter exercises of the imagination. Many excellent judges, I know, have a great stomach for it; they delight in symbols and correspondences, in seeing a story told as if it were another and a very different story. I frankly confess that I have as a general thing but little enjoyment of it, and that it has never seemed to me to be, as it were, a first-rate literary form. . . . It is apt to spoil two good things—a story and a moral, a meaning and a form; and the taste for it is responsible for a large part of the forcible-feeble writing that has been inflicted upon the world." Apart from noting once again the identification of allegory and example ("a moral"), one finishes that quotation with the feeling of having just read an epitaph. Is this, then, the end? Can nothing be said in praise of allegory?

Allegory as Play

If that citation from Henry James reads like epitaph, the following must stand against it as epigraph. "We seem to have moved from an open-ended, anthropocentric, humanistic, naturalistic, even—to the extent that man may be thought of as making his own universe—optimistic starting point, to one that is closed, cosmic, eternal, supernatural (in its soberest sense), and pessimistic. The return to Being has returned us to Design, to microcosmic images of the macrocosm, to the creation of Beauty within the confines of cosmic or human necessity, to the use of the fabulous to probe beyond the phenomenological, beyond appearances, beyond randomly perceived events, beyond mere history. But these probes are above all—like your Knight's sallies—challenges to the assumptions of a dying age, exemplary adventures of the Poetic Imagination, high-minded journeys toward the New World and never mind that the nag's a pile of bones." The words are from Robert Coover's superb "Dedicatoria y Prólogo a don Miguel de Cervantes Saavedra," which prefaces his "Seven Exemplary Fictions" in *Pricksongs and Descants*. It is time, it would seem, to take another look at allegory.

I have selected a very short parable of Franz Kafka as a case study and, once again, I am very indebted to the analysis of Heinz Politzer. In order not to prejudice the discussion by a summary I quote the story in full.

It was very early in the morning, the streets clean and deserted, I was on my way to the railroad station. As I compared the tower clock with my watch I realized it was already much later than I had thought. I had to hurry, the shock of this discovery made me feel uncertain of the way, I was not very well acquainted with the town as yet, fortunately there was a policeman nearby, I ran to him and breathlessly asked him the way. He smiled and said: "From me you want to learn the way?" "Yes," I said, "since I cannot find it myself."

"Give it up, give it up," said he, and turned away with a great sweep, like someone who wants to be alone with his laughter.

Imagine, as adapted from Politzer, some different interpretations or variant readings of this story. They are representative rather than restrictive. There could be more and even these tend to mingle with one another.

In an *autobiographical* reading the policeman is Kafka's father and this can be backed up quite convincingly with quotations from his 1919 *Letter to His Father*. A *psychological* reading sees the story as an image of acute neurasthenia in which the patient's search cannot find either the right time or the right place and ends in frozen immobility. (I spare you phallic clocktowers, etc.) A *sociological* reading might discuss the claustrophobic trap of the ghetto in which a Jewish community was immersed in a Slav city like Prague. An *historical* reading would emphasize the ineffectual police power of the Hapsburg monarchy which had been overthrown some time before the story was written. A *metaphysical* reading might see in the policeman's refusal to arbitrate direction the waning power of philosophy to answer the questions posed to it. And a *religious* reading could find in the policeman's silence a vision of the death of God. With analytic imagination and interpretive sensitivity any or all of those readings could be argued most persuasively. And so no doubt could many more we cannot even envisage at present.

What conclusions can be drawn from the above discussion? First, the story defies singularity or univocity in its interpretation. Second, the story demands plurality and multiplicity in its reading. Third, and most important, the story itself is a metaphor for those first two points taken together. What does the story mean, where is *the* correct interpretation. The only answer, and this comes from the story itself, is: "Give up" that question, "Give up" that search. The policeman in the story is the story about the policeman. Allegory allegorizes allegory. The story always has the last laugh.

Notice, however, that it is not a question of multiple interpretations on the same level as in the various possible solutions to a murder mystery. It is a question of multiple levels of interpretation on each and all of which the story makes excellent sense, levels which range from personal to social, from psychological to sociological, and from philosophical to theological.

I think that this gives us a helpful insight into allegory in its most intrinsic and challenging dimensions. An allegory is a story whose plurality of interpretive levels indicates that the original is itself a metaphor for that multiplicity. The multiple levels of reading do not derive from authorial indecision, linguistic incompetence, or critical misapprehension. These various levels developed by analysis are but the obedient reflection of the multiplicity imaged in and by the story itself.

This can be illustrated from a more contemporary allegory, the beautiful and beguiling novel *The Last Unicorn* by Peter S. Beagle. And I believe in unicorns when novels can open like this: "The unicorn lived in a lilac wood, and she lived all alone. She was very old, though she did not know it, and she was no longer the careless color of sea foam, but rather the color of snow falling on a moonlit night. But her eyes were still clear and unwearied, and she still moved like a shadow on the sea." The major protagonists are the White Unicorn and the Red Bull and the story concerns the Unicorn's quest to free her fellows from the power of the Bull. I leave it totally to your imagination to interpret the story on all the varied levels suggested earlier for Kafka's parable. But the ultimate victory of the White Unicorn consists in being joined with a myriad of her kind from out the sea where the Bull had trapped them in the whitecaps. And it is the Red Bull who departs into the depths of the sea, and who departs there all alone. The magic of multiplicity is set against the tyranny of univocity in the story and so also in the interpretation. This is also the morality of the story. There is none of the usual reinforcement of standard virtue or punishment for standard vice which has made allegory almost synonymous with example and about as desirable as well.

This, then, is what allegory is all about at its best and deepest level. Allegory is plot at play. It makes us aware that one single story containing one single plot can be read on every level we can imagine, from the most personally private to the most cosmically transcendent. It reveals the relativity of plot not only within the novel itself but across all the realms of world and of reality. Why be surprised, it asks us, to discover that the way we structure an autobiography may be exactly how we structure an epoch, or that private life and public theology may have a similar or isomorphic structuration. But here now is a most important parting of the ways. At another time and in another place this would have been explained, as I noted earlier, in terms of divine design and divine purpose. In this time and in this place I find another conclusion more compellingly imperative. It is the structuring processes of the human imagination which is at work in *all* these levels of interpretative possibility. It is the same imagination, the same playful human imagination, which is at work in fiction, in history, and in philosophy, and what wonder then if it can produce a single plot which can be read on all these variant levels.

Allegory is the laughter of plot, the triumphant laughter of the human imagination at play with plot and in plot. As Mikhail Bakhtin put it, "Laughter purifies from dogmatism, from the intolerant and the petrified; it liberates from fanaticism and pedantry, from fear and intimidation, from didacticism, naïveté and illusion, *from the single meaning, the single level*, from sentimentality" (my italics).

There are many devices to reveal the necessity and the relativity of plot in works of fiction and I mentioned earlier the extravagant praise lavished by Victor Shklovsky on Sterne's *Tristram Shandy* for precisely this aspect of its artistic creativity. Allegory, however, goes much deeper than this because it reveals to our startled eyes the ubiquity and universality of plot across all the creativity of the playful human imagination, from autobiography to theology and from psychology to philosophy. "Because men have seen no unicorns for a while does not mean they have all vanished."

Parables and Allegories

In classical allegory it made little difference whether one dealt with two clear levels in the story or admitted the possibility of multiple meanings. Medieval exegesis, for example, could give the Bible readings almost as diverse and as interesting as Politzer recorded for Kafka's discussed earlier. But meanings however multiple or readings however diverse were all held in structured harmony as layers of divine causality and one could climb by analogy to their common source in God. This made allegory and example so intertwined that moral or exemplaric allegory is almost tautologous. What God did was the most precise and imperative model for human action and conduct and all those layers of medieval exegesis were fraught with both ethical admonition and moral persuasion.

A contemporary theory of allegory and a modern reading of ancient allegory has no such security and no such serenity. Multiplicity now bespeaks the inevitability of imaginative structurations and hence their isomorphic relationships and if one invokes transcendence in such a situation it must be found not by a climb in light but rather by a leap in darkness, not as the Topmost Rung but as Altogether Off Our Ladder. This means that allegory in a contemporary reading will no longer be securely bonded to example but will appear much more wedded to parable. Its multiplicity will no longer be that of reiterated example but that of insoluble paradox. Allegory, to borrow from Roland Barthes in another context, is not an apricot with a stone set in its centre and we in search of that stone, but an onion whose manifold layers constitute its totality and whose multiplicity is its message. We have been taught, of course, to prefer apricots to onions.

When allegory is understood in this contemporary sense it is quite possible to discuss Borges as both a parabler and an allegorist. No matter at what level his stories are read, the paradox is still there. And this is axiomatic. An allegorical parable retains the paradox at the heart of every reading. When the paradox disappears in any reading we have slipped into an allegorical example. What then of Jesus?

As in all previous cases I presume a fundamental distinction between what Jesus' language said and what the present interpretive frames of the tradition's transmission record for us. Jesus' stories were parables, narrative paradoxes, and if they are read allegorically that original paradox should still be there on any and every level of reading.

The tradition formulated its theory of interpretation in brilliant fashion in Mark 4. The story of "The Sower" tells how a farmer suffers three types of loss as the seed is destroyed by birds, rocks, or thorns, and juxtaposes this with three degrees of success as the harvest yields thirty, sixty, or even a hundred grains to the ear. This is then explained as a *separation* and/or *opposition* allegory necessitated by opposition to Jesus' message and forcing him to speak obliquely. The purpose is to prevent profanation of the message and persecution of the messenger. But then the story is clearly explained to the insiders and its moral message becomes quite obvious. There are those who fail to accept the word of God and there are those who accept it totally. I suppose the other two motives are also present. When the results of Christian preaching are in such obvious harmony with the data of agricultural experience persuasive *continuation* is established and the divine *structuration* of nature and of history is revealed. As *an* interpretation of the story one can hardly deny its cogency and its validity but as *the* interpretation precluding all others it domesticates permanently and thereby destroys completely the paradox of gain-in-loss and loss-in-gain which is at the heart of the story's abrupt juxtaposition of losses and gains, of sowing failure and harvest plenitude. In fact Jesus' story puts in narrative format the paradox seen already among his counterproverbs: Who loses life, saves it; who saves, loses it. Does the tradition's interpretation maintain that paradox or does it convert it into the reassuring truism that you lose a few to win a few, or lose a few, win a lot? My answer would be that it has changed from the paradoxical simultaneity of a loss/gain equation into the proverbial succession of a loss/gain sequence. Allegorical parable has become allegorical example.

It is amusing to note the difficulty the tradition had in making its exemplaric interpretation fit the story. It worked brilliantly on the three degrees of loss with the birds as Satan, the rocks as persecution, and the thorns as temptation. But what then of the three degrees of gain? If the losses were Christians who fell from faith, would not the three *levels* of gain be those who stayed? There would then be three levels of Christians in the community. Mark 4:20 ignored the problem. Matt 13:23 was quite willing to accept but not explicitate this interpretation since he constantly evinces throughout his Gospel severe doubts about the final fate of certain Christians within his own community. So he reverses Mark's order to underline the point that there are "in one case a hundredfold, in another sixty, and in another thirty" degree Christians among even the insiders. Note the descending degrees. Thom 9 simplifies the problem by moving from three to two degrees: "It bore sixty per measure and one hundred twenty per measure." But as in so many other cases it is Luke 8:8 who is the most ruthless critic. He solves the problem by eliminating completely any degrees of gain: "And some fell into good soil and grew, and yielded a hundredfold." No degrees of gain and therefore no problem of degrees among Christian believers.

There are three features of this inaugural and paradigmatic model for the "proper reading" of Jesus' stories which should be noted. First, an allegorical parable will generate interpretations that are both *multiple* and *paradoxical*. While any given interpretation may maintain that it is the best, fullest, or most interesting reading, and while this can always be tolerated and argued as a phenomenon of human play (exegetes have a right to play just as much as artists), the paradox at the heart of parable must never be omitted in any interpretation. Jesus' story has been given a canonically correct reading and as far as I can see there is no paradox in its explanation in Mark 4. To say that one must have losses before or alongside gains *is not the same as* to claim that losses are gains and gains losses. On the other hand, the paradox seems to be retained in a text such as that of John 12:24, "Truly, truly, I say to you, unless a grain of wheat falls into the earth and dies, it remains alone; but if it dies, it bears much fruit." Second, the interpretation has been appended externally and separately so that the story itself has not been tampered with internally. Three, this is a moral allegory derived from a natural or agricultural story. These last two features may explain the rather dismal failure of the tradition's allegorical reading of other stories of Jesus where the reading is not externally added but internally inserted and where the allegory is not moral but historical.

For example. Jesus' story of "The Evil Tenants" is a lethal trickster story in which an absentee landlord thinks his tenants will not recognize a servant's power to collect the rent and sends his only son instead. His stupidity results in the son's murder so that the tenants can inherit the vineyard by default. The text closest to Jesus' original may still be seen in Thom 65. The tradition strove mightily to turn this into an historical allegory of the process of salvation leading to the death of Jesus. It is the sort of attempt that has given allegory a bad name. It simply will not work because resurrection will not fit into that original story as it was never intended to be read there in the first place. Read the allegorization in Matt 21:33–44 and ask yourself if the following description by Edwin Honig applies here. "A good allegory . . . beguiles the reader with a continuous interplay between subject and sense in the storytelling, and the narrative, the story itself, means everything." The problem in Matt 21:33–44 is that it is bad allegory not because allegory is intrinsically bad or because Matthew is incompetent, but because he has inherited a story that simply cannot be allegorized into the interpretation he needs. It is not that the diverse readings of an allegory must agree with some original paradigmatic interpretation but that isomorphic plotting must be present at every level of interpretation. And note that, in this case, the interpretation is internally inserted into the story itself, and that the story does not concern nature but history. But once again one can turn to Luke 20:9–18 which recognizes that the story has become problematic and attempts to simplify it into more credible format.

The point of this discussion is that Jesus' stories are parables, narrative paradoxes, which can be read on many different levels of interpretation as long as their core paradox is constantly affirmed. They cannot be given one normative reading, whether that canonical interpretation be historical or moral, whether it details what God has done or we must do in the struggle for salvation. Except, of course, where a normative interpretation is simply a challenge for others to join in hermeneutic play but within the strict rules of isomorphic structuration.

Jesus and Borges are both parablers. They can be read allegorically on whatever semantic level or in whatever systematic discipline one pleases but without destroying or evading the paradox that must constantly recur at every stratum and in every interpretation. In this sense, then, "The Stone Fisherman" by Bertolt Brecht can be taken as a parable of parables:

> The big fisherman has appeared again. He sits in his rotted boat and fishes from the time when the first lamps flare up early in the morning until the last one is put out in the evening.
>
> The villagers sit on the gravel of the embankment and watch him, grinning. He fishes for herring but he pulls up nothing but stones.
>
> They all laugh. The men slap their sides, the women hold on to their bellies, the children leap high into the air with laughter.
>
> When the big fisherman raises his torn net high and finds the stones in it, he does not hide them but reaches far out with his strong brown arms. seizes the stone, holds it high and shows it to the unlucky ones.

Fourth Variation:
Time and Finitude

> Time is the substance I am made of. Time is a river which sweeps me along, but I am the river; it is a tiger which destroys me, but I am the tiger; it is a fire which consumes me, but I am the fire.
>
> Jorge Luis Borges

This Variation turns from genre to theme, to the phenomenon of time as a very basic problem for both Jesus and Borges. With Borges it is explicitly underlined and repeatedly stressed but with Jesus its importance and indeed its very existence has to be demonstrated. Time appears in Jesus' stories and aphorisms according to the principle of Ts'ui Pên's novel *The Garden of the Forking Paths* in Borges's story of the same name: "[This novel] is an enormous guessing game, or parable, in which the subject is time. The rules of the game forbid the use of the word itself. To eliminate a word completely, to refer to it by means of inept phrases and obvious paraphrases, is perhaps the best way of drawing attention to it." With Jesus, as distinct, from Borges, I shall have to consider something neither mentioned directly nor named explicitly.

1. TIME

Courtesy and custom dictate that I open the discussion with Augustine's famous paradox from Book 11 of his *Confessions*. "What, then, is time? If no one asks of me, I know; if I wish to explain to him who asks, I know not." Some distinctions may assist in making more precise exactly what is the problem of time not only as Augustine saw it but as it still appears for us today.

Six Distinctions

We know immediately the difference between *sidereal* and *experiential* time so this can be a first distinction to introduce the subject. By sidereal time I mean the time established by watch and clock, by chronometer and calendar. We have learned to read such measurements correctly, but we have also learned that experiential time need not coincide with their peremptory imperialism. Time drags or time passes swiftly. We subjectively experience the passage of objective time as being far swifter or far slower than the clock records. This leads to a second distinction, that between *empty* and *filled* time. When we experience sidereal time as dragging it is because we are bored or uninterested or unoccupied, because those objective slots are not filled with subjective concentration or enjoyment. When time is filled or fulfilled we wish to arrest even its objective passage and say that hours are like minutes and other such profundities. So, a third distinction, and here the problem starts to become much more difficult. Filled time can be considered as either *individual* and private or as *epochal* and public. We know that an individual's time can become absolutely filled with a private concern so that the person is described as living for that interest alone. But apart from such solipsistic fulfillment of one's time there is also the more problematic phenomenon of epochal time. How are the empty slots of sidereal time filled and fulfilled on levels that go beyond simple individual preoccupations. And what are those levels? Next, a fourth distinction, still more difficult. Are these epochs of shared and communal fulfillment *disunited* and without mutual connection or are they somehow *united* each with the other in some overarching design.

With the help of these first four distinctions which should be taken as successive and subsidiary, I would state the core problem of time, the fulfilled time of human temporality, in this question: How is epochal time unified? For the major answers to this question I depend primarily on certain papers given during the "Eranos" meetings of 1949 and 1951 at Lake Maggiore in Switzerland. These were published in 1957 as *Man and Time* and it is the best single volume on the subject that I know about at the moment.

One answer to that core problem just enunciated is given in the paper "Primordial Time and Final Time" by the Dutch philosopher of religion Gerardus van der Leeuw. The passage adds a fifth distinction to the series of four already given above.

> Here we approach the great cleavage in the self-consciousness of mankind. On the one side, time takes a cyclical course, on the other it has a beginning before which there was nothing and an end with which it stops. On the one side, every sunrise is a victory over chaos, every festival a cosmic beginning, every sowing a new creation, every holy place a foundation or fall according to the regular course of the world, and even the law that sustains society is nothing other than the rule of the sun's course. . . . On the other side, everything is exactly the same except that at a certain point in the cycle someone appears who proclaims a definitive event, the day of Yahweh, the last judgment, the ultimate salvation, or the final conflict as in Iran.

The article by Henri-Charles Puech of the Sorbonne specifies this great cleavage (my fifth distinction) between *cyclical* and *linear* time by noting that

> the Greek world conceived of time as above all cyclical or circular, returning perpetually upon itself, self-enclosed, under the influence of astronomical movements which command and regulate its course with necessity. For Christianity, on the contrary, time is bound up with the Creation and continuous action of God; it unfolds unilaterally in one direction, beginning at a single source and aiming toward a single goal: it is oriented and represents a progression from the past toward the future; it is one, organic and progressive; consequently it has a full reality.

It must be noted that certain presuppositions seem to accompany this fifth distinction of time circular and time linear. First, that these options supply the major or fundamental possibilities. Second, that a linear is somehow better than a circular understanding. Third, and most important, that the line has both beginning and end, that the end is construed as teleological goal or purpose, and that in between there is both progress and improvement.

At this point we begin to discern a sixth distinction in which we ask whether this line of teleological continuity and ultimate purpose is given to us, be it by God or evolution, or is created by us in and from our human imagination. There is a glimpse of this question at the very end of van der Leeuw's article where he says that modern science has rejected circular time because "it sees the process of development as linear and unrepeatable, but on principle without eschatology, without meaning and purpose." Note the univocal sense of eschatology as *the* ending of *this* world and the presumption that lack of such ending is equivalent to absence of meaning and loss of purpose. But surely we need a sixth distinction here between a *progressive* linear teleology where the ending and the meaning and the purpose are all synonymous and a *discrete* linear eschatology whose multiple endings challenge us to a different sense of meaning and of purpose. In visual imagery linear can designate both an ascending and continuous graph or a horizontal but broken and disconnected line.

Star-time or Story-time

Helmuth Plessner might be expected to sympathize with a circular theory of time since the Nazis who had dismissed him from his philosophy chair at Göttingen in 1933 did it again in 1943 from Groningen in Holland. But it is his article, "On the Relation of Time to Death," which raises most explicitly this sixth distinction which I have just mentioned.

Is the idea of an absolute meaning one of man's vital needs? Can he exist only in a directed time, once it has dawned on him that time is essentially alien to space? Can he cast off the heritage of eschatological thinking? Can he cease to ask after a meaning, aim, or purpose, without confronting death as nothingness? Are we reduced to the alternative of a renewal of Christian transcendence—that is, the eschatological picture of time—or of the flight from time into a mythical view of eternal recurrence?

You will recognize that we are right back in my First Variation's section on "The Ending of Cosmic Plan" where I used the term comic eschatology to question and to doubt the absolute validity of any cosmic teleology. Comic eschatology reminds us that it is our imagination which fills time with meaning and thereby creates both time and ourselves. Van der Leeuw himself had asserted that,

We can live with clocks, angles, and square feet, and all these are assuredly necessary. Except that we cannot actually *live* by them. When one says space and time, one means one's own life. That is, one means not empty surface, not a chronometer, but myth. Time is favored time: the dividing lines have been made on the basis of life's experiencs. Time is full, and its content is the myths—that is, the forms of life that lie heaped up for all time in the womb of the unconscious.

I would rephrase this in my own earlier terminology by saying that fulfilled time is story and must therefore be a dialectic of myth and parable so that the latter keeps the former honest and aware that even our most magnificent constructions of fulfilled time, for example the Christian myth of progression from primordial to final time, is no more and no less than just that—a magnificent construct of the human imagination in which we lived quite happily and most successfully for a very long span of sidereal time.

A story and especially a superstory assists the coherent establishment of the past's continuity and the future's projection. When story or superstory (myth) breaks down or maybe just becomes boring we move into another story and, looking backward from the clarity of the new, we attempt to show the causal continuity between the two stories. Time is, then, an absolutely necessary and humanly inevitable concomitant of story. It is the imagination's play with layers of story within which and only within which we live, move, and have our being.

We know as an obvious truism that I can tell you a family saga extending over ten years in five minutes and, conversely, I could tell you the events of a catastrophic few seconds in a story lasting all day. It is a subtle warning that star-time and story-time need not coincide. And that is exactly the distinction with which I started this section. We know that sidereal and experiential time do not coincide. That was my opening comment. I would now explain that by claiming that we live with star-time but in story-time and every child knows that these two times have very little to do with each other. We tell stories and we live stories and the time of neither coincides with the metric time of the wheeling stars. And that, I would submit, is just too bad for the stars. As Schmendrick said to Molly in Beagle's *The Last Unicorn*, "Haven't you ever been in a fairy tale before?"

2. CIRCLE

I shall begin with Borges, against the background of the preceding introductory section, and recalling especially what was said there concerning circular time.

Borges on Time

With Borges time is expressly presented as a problem. It is cited in his interviews, discussed in his essays, mentioned in his poems, and appears centrally both in the content and form of many of his stories.

When he was being interviewed at New York University's Washington Square campus on April 8, 1971, he answered Norman Thomas di Giovanni's question on space by talking of time, "I tend to be always thinking of time, not of space. . . . I think that the central problem of metaphysics—let us call it thinking—is time not space. . . . I think the real problem, the problem we have to grapple with, and of course the problem whose solution we'll never find, is the problem of time, of successive time, and, therein, the problem of personal identity, which is but a part of the problem of time."

His most famous article on the subject is a combination of two essays from 1944 and 1946 now juxtaposed and ironically titled, "New Refutation of Time." Here is the heart of the argument. "I deny, with the arguments of idealism, the vast temporal series which idealism admits. Hume denied the existence of an absolute space, in which all things have their place; I deny the existence of one single time, in which all things are linked as in a chain. The denial of coexistence is no less arduous than the denial of succession." That at least is clear. Time is our invention, carved by our imagination and complete in all its imaginary linkages.

Time appears again in two poems from 1968 and once again there is an equation between our being and our time. In "Heraclitus" he repeats a line he had used to close the above essay twenty years before, and which I quoted as epigraph for this Variation.

> The river bears me on and I am the river.
> I was made of a changing substance, of mysterious time.

It is a cliché to say that time is a river, but what if one adds that I am that river? A similar equation is made between time past and time present, between memory and identity, in "Cambridge."

> We are our memory
> we are this chimerical museum of shifting forms,
> this heap of broken mirrors.

And, finally, there are the stories. It is easy to point to time within story content, to quotations such as these from "The Garden of Forking Paths." Talking of Ts'ui Pên, Stephen Albert says, "I know that of all problems, none disturbed him so greatly nor worked upon him so much as the abysmal problem of time." And what is the solution he discovered? "In contrast to Newton and Schopenhauer [he] did not believe in a uniform, absolute time. He believed in an infinite series of times, in a growing, dizzying net of divergent, convergent and parallel times." That must suffice for time in the content of a story as I wish to give some attention to time in the form of a story and this is of much more significance.

For a case study I shall take the 1952 tale "The Man on the Threshold." As noted so often before in Borges an Author-I (a friend of Borges's real-life friend Bioy-Casares!) cedes place after the opening paragraph to a Narrator-I. This narrator, one Christopher Dewey, arrives, in the days of Empire, to investigate the sudden disappearance of the British official who had successfully if violently subdued the turmoil of Sikh and Muslim in an Indian city. He makes absolutely no progress in his search until, "One afternoon, I was handed an envelope containing a slip of paper on which there was an address." Arriving at the house after sunset he finds that "some kind of Muslim ceremony was being held" and stops to question an ancient beggar squatting on the threshold. "The old man did not understand me (perhaps he did not hear me), and I had to explain that Glencairn was a judge and that I was looking for him." And now comes a third or Character-I as the old man takes over and Dewey has to listen to the fate of one Nicholson "that happened when I was a boy." He was a British judge who had become as corrupt and venal as those he prosecuted. He was finally kidnapped, all those he had wronged were gathered as witnesses, and as judge was chosen a madman "so that God's wisdom might speak through his mouth and shame human pride." Dewey asks how long the trial lasted; the ancient answers "at least nineteen days" but is corrected by a man leaving the Muslim ceremony in the inner court, "Nineteen days—exactly." Dewey forces his way inside through the crowd now emerging and sees a naked man whose "sword was stained, for it had dealt Glencairn his death. I found his mutilated body in the stables out back."

Borges has elsewhere called this "a bit of a trick story and a game with time." It is, of course, both, but it is also revelatory of more fundamental and inevitable tricks with story and games with time. Borges continues, "What is told as having happened years and years earlier is actually taking place at the moment. The teller, of course, as he patiently spins his yarn, is really hindering the officer from breaking in and stopping the trial and the execution." The ancient's story is true only if, and as long as Dewey stays and listens to it. His story is history.

What is at stake in all this probing of time is both personal identity and objective reality. Ana María Barrenechea has said that, "To undermine the reader's belief in the concreteness of life, Borges attacks those fundamental concepts on which the security of living itself is founded: the universe, personality and time."

Circular Time

Jorge Rodrigo Ayora concluded his 1969 Vanderbilt dissertation on time theories in Borges by stating that, "The preponderant one is the theory of the Eternal Return or cyclic time, which is practically omnipresent in one form or another in all his production." Most commentators would agree. Ronald Christ, for example, quotes Borges' statement, "I am accustomed to return eternally to the Eternal Return," from the opening of "Circular Time" in his 1936 collection *Historia de la eternidad*, which has never been translated into English. But Ayora has added an important comment on Borges's predilection for circular time, for that time sense more reminiscent of the Greek than of the Christian roots of Western consciousness. He asks why Borges "who as a writer has always insisted on being as universal as possible, disregards the largest body of quasi-universal mythology and symbology common to Western man, the Bible"? His answer is that Borges cannot accept the biblical view of time. "Borges's temperament as a man and artist has no affinity with a conception of time that in the final analysis is finite, limited at both beginning and end, has a definite 'forward' direction, and is optimistic in outlook." I leave aside for the moment the question whether the biblical view is as monolithic and teleological as Christian interpretation has led us to believe. Ayora's point is an acute observation on Borges's almost total silence concerning the Bible. The few exceptions serve only to underline the general silence.

And yet, and yet . . . at the end of "The Library of Babel" the narrator says this of its vast bibliocosmic disorder. "If an eternal voyager were to traverse it in any direction, he would find, after many centuries, that the same volumes are repeated in the same disorder (which repeated, would constitute an order: Order itself). My solitude rejoices in this elegant hope." But when Borges comes to form this elegant hope into plot the circularity is not exactly perfect. Recall "Pierre Menard, Author of the *Quixote*." Pierre Menard had managed to reproduce a section of Cervantes's novel with verbatim fidelity. Surely here is time's circularity in at least one explicit example.

But instead the narrator reminds us how totally different is our reading and understanding of this same text coming from the twentieth as opposed to the seventeenth century. "It is not in vain that three hundred years have passed, charged with the most complex happenings—among them, to mention only one, that same *Don Quixote*." Time's circularity is differentiated at least in that a *re*petition is not the original petition. It was formally easier to equate story and event in "The Man on the Threshold" than to show cyclic identity in "Pierre Menard."

What emerges preponderantly from Borges is not so much a positive acceptance of circular time as a negative probing of the weaknesses of linear or biblical time. Circularity serves as a comic and parabolic critique of our presumption that linear and progressive time, be it in Christian apocalypse or in secular utopia, is an obvious and self-evident datum of objective reality. Once again I quote in conclusion from Ana María Barrenechea. "To the reader who is comfortably installed in life, Borges has shown the perturbing spectacle of the inverse temporal flow, of the presently existing future, of a life which is wholly in the past, and of a past which is illusory or easy to erase or transformable at will."

The Circle of Play

There is, however, another way in which Borges's preoccupation with circular time's eternal return can be placed in conjunction with the time experiments in his stories. Jaime Alazraki has written that, "of all the versions of the eternal return, Borges seems to enjoy most the one that considers the cycles which repeat themselves infinitely not as identical but as similar." How are we to conceptualize such cycles of similarity without identity?

For my answer I am indebted to Lawrence M. Hinman's article on "Nietzsche's Philosophy of Play" in *Philosophy Today* for Summer 1974. His point is "how Nietzsche's view of man and the world is based on one fundamental insight into the play character of existence," and this is of present importance because, expectedly, Borges discussed Nietzsche's theory of the eternal return in that early article on "Circular Time."

In *Thus Spoke Zarathustra* Nietzsche said, "Of three metamorphoses of the spirit I tell you: How the spirit becomes a camel; and the camel, a lion; and the lion, finally, a child." The ascendancy of the child derives from the fact that the child is "a game . . . the game of creation." The child is the one who utters the "sacred 'Yes' " which "conquers his own world," which creates the world as play, in play, and by play. Hinman cites as well the passage from Book Five of *The Joyful Wisdom* where "The Great Health" is described. "Another ideal runs on before us, a strange, tempting ideal, full of danger, to which we should not like to persuade any one, because we do not readily acknowledge any one's *right thereto*: the ideal of a spirit who plays naively (that is to say involuntarily and from overflowing abundance and power) with everything that has hitherto been called holy, good, inviolable, divine."

Play as the supreme human activity gathers the major emphases of Nietzsche's philosophy into a unity. Hinman summarizes: "If the will to power represents the idea of creative play, and the overman is seen as representing man's possibility of becoming the player in this eternal game, then the doctrine of eternal recurrence of the same expresses the play-character of the world which the overman creates through his will to power." Time's circularity or the eternal return does not mean that the same earlier event happens in exact but later duplication. Eternal return, in Hinman's understanding of Nietzsche, "does not mean that the content of each and every moment must be the same, but rather that the structure of each moment is the same insofar as each moment is a moment of play." As any player of a beloved game knows full well, it is always the same over and over again but it is also always different over and over again.

The symbol which has become synonymous with Borges is the *labyrinth* and it may serve as a visual cipher for the eternal return but conceived as joyful and creative play. For most commentators this is usually taken as a symbol of doom and of dread even if most recognize that it is not unmitigated hopelessness. Take, for example, three articles spanning a decade of criticism and all having the term labyrinth in their titles. In

1959 L. A. Murillo concluded that, "From within the hollows of his labyrinths, Borges echoes that postscript of our age by which we manage to survive: not until now has man known himself to be such an odd creature that, in his deepest despair, despair may be a comfort to him." Once again, in 1962, H. E. Lewald admits that, "Although the sequence of chaos-hopelessness-futility forms the core of many of his stories, we do not find the expected note of despair, so customary in modern writers whose ontological and moral structure has collapsed." Finally, in 1969, N. D. Isaacs, even though insisting that "the labyrinth is a symbol of art" concludes that, "The labyrinth, as archetypal symbol of artifice, is maddening (literally) perhaps only because of the ultimate futility of the gestures of art, the falsefaced rituals of patterned humanity."

The negativity which breathes through all these interpretations of labyrinth in Borges presumes one or both of two suppositions and thus makes them the end of the past rather than the beginning of the future. They presuppose that one enters a labyrinth to attain some desired center and/or one wishes to exit eventually from the maze. But what if there is no center and therefore no content therein? And what if one has not the slightest desire to exit the labyrinth? What if there is only labyrinth and if the labyrinth is play and if it is our play that built and builds the labyrinth itself? It is here that Nietzsche and Borges seem to meet most completely. Circular time is the repetitious time of creative play for Nietzsche and the time of labyrinth building and exploration for Borges. Play is a beauty ever ancient and ever new, long have we loved it, but far too late have we admitted its inevitability and ubiquity.

3. LINE

Augustine spoke for the Christian *via recta* of linear time against the *circuitus* of Neoplatonic circular time when, in Book 12 of *The City of God*, he challenged "these arguments, with which the impious seek to turn our simple faith away from the straight way, in order that we may walk in a circle with them." But the biblical data was more complicated than he imagined. (The biblical data is always more complicated than anyone imagines.) One recalls the sardonic comment of G. Quispel: "I have never been able to find a single important doctrine in Augustine which is not based on an error in Bible translation."

Prophecy and Apocalyptic

There is still rather intense scholarly debate on the continuity and discontinuity, the similarities and the differences between pre-exilic prophecy and the later postexilic apocalyptic writings inside and outside the Hebrew Bible. I shall limit myself here to what is of immediate relevance and thereby avoid getting into more trouble than is absolutely necessary.

Both the prophetic and the apocalyptic imagination presume some linear continuity and causality between present and future and both speak a message to the immediate present in view of future divine action. But what seems to me to be the essential difference is that the prophetic vision had no idea of an afterlife and no conception of a "heaven" where the elect might live forever with their God. The apocalyptic seer, however, could stand in the midst of terrible persecution, proleptic Holocaust, and proclaim in hope that "thou shalt look from on high and shalt see thy enemies in Gehenna" as in *The Testament of Moses* 10:10. Prophecy and apocalyptic had both to look into the heart of darkness and find beyond it a gleam of hope. But there is an important difference between the prophetic eschatology which envisages *a* world coming to *an* end and the apocalyptic eschatology which spoke of *this* world coming to *the* end. No matter how world-shattering might be the coming catastrophe, the prophet could not imagine the ending of world unless God were to abrogate and repent creation, and no prophet was quite ready to proclaim that eternal silence. But the apocalyptic seer could very easily announce this world's dissolution since there was another one where righteousness might dwell at peace and the elect find comfort for the persecution they had endured from evil here below. Scholarship has always emphasized this close connection between persecution and apocalyptic and I am inclined to think that, the more real and present the persecution, the more literally was the language of imminent deliverance accepted by those who heard or read its promises. In other words, the imminence usually associated with apocalyptic scenarios is an important but secondary feature of this primary assurance that, despite the horror and injustice of persecution here below, there are sanctions beyond this life, there is justice at least beyond the grave.

Immortality as Idolatry

At this point it is only fair to declare my own position on this problem so you can be aware where personal presuppositions may be at work in hidden ways. Since I presume that those who work without presuppositions are usually found enjoying bananas in the treetops it does not bother me to confess my own principles as an invitation to others to do likewise. In "The Three Versions of Judas" Borges put it this way: "Someone may observe that no doubt the conclusion preceded the 'proofs.' For who gives himself up to looking for proofs for something he does not believe in or the predication of which he does not care about?"

Here, then, is my problem and my presupposition. Why did Israel so long and so firmly resist any concept of immortality, eternal life, reincarnation, or any idea which negates the terminal finitude of death as the end of individual human existence? For my present purpose I make no distinction between immortality as intrinsic correlative of the soul and eternal life as divine gift for the faithful individual.

Religions can compose both myths of Beginning and myths of Ending. Israel showed herself eminently capable of taking over myths of beginning from Mesopotamian civilization and adapting them to the ethical monotheism of her own God as is so amply demonstrated by the opening chapters of Genesis. Why, then, did she never accept with similar discretion the myths of Ending from Egypt with which she also had constant contact? Indeed, it would seem easier to adapt their concept of eternal sanctions for earthly actions than to have made all the necessary ethical changes in taking over Mesopotamian myth.

For example, the 125th chapter of the Egyptian "Book of the Dead" would seem quite at home in Israel. "I have given bread to the hungry, water to the thirsty, clothing to the naked, and a ferry-boat to him who was marooned." I am quite well aware that I am offering an argument from absence and from silence. But the lack of any concept of immortality or eternal life in ancient Israel demands some explanation both in its Near Eastern setting and also against the wider background of the history of religions. I do not deny that Israel evinced what might best be described as a poetry of the tomb but such is not a song of immortality. Why this strange silence?

I consider this a very serious problem and my own explanation of it is that Israel considered any idea of immortality or eternal life as inherently and irredeemably idolatrous. The individual might imagine children and children's children living on among the living people of God but the individual accepted personal mortality as both inevitable and ineluctable. To claim or even ask for more was to encroach on the prerogatives of divinity itself.

Since I presume this to have been the prophetic understanding of death I am convinced that the arrival of belief in personal immortality was for Israel breakdown rather than breakthrough in her faith in God. One can almost see it happen on both the individual and national levels. On the individual level the older claims of Proverbs 10:3 that, "The Lord does not let the righteous go hungry, but he thwarts the craving of the wicked," are denied on theoretical grounds by Ecclesiastes and on practical grounds by Job. Divine justice such as that of Proverbs does not exist on earth. But the dilemma will be "solved" by the book of Wisdom which declares that divine justice is sanctioned not here but hereafter for "the souls of the righteous are in the hands of God . . . their hope is full of immortality" (3:1, 4). On the national level, as well, the experience of reiterated and hopeless persecution which is the background for apocalyptic led most understandably to a belief that God had abandoned this evil age and that only in a hopefully imminent hereafter would divine justice be vindicated.

My criticism is not really with those who forged this theology of afterlife in the crucible of persecution but rather with those who, in calmer days, accepted it all uncritically as somehow self-evidently magnificent. (I take it that the procedures used in abandoning the *Titanic* did not become normative for later Cunard dockings in Southampton and New York.)

Robert Frost has rephrased this question in "A Steeple on the House,"

> What if it should turn out eternity
> Was but the steeple on our house of life
> That made our house of life a house of worship?
> We do not go up there to sleep at night.
> We do not go up there to live by day.
> Nor need we ever go out there to live.
> A spire and belfry coming on the roof
> Means that a soul is coming on the flesh.

I am unable to accept the afterlife of apocalyptic vision except as a crisis-response, a narcotic theology to stop the pain of meaningless suffering and of hopeless persecution. but, as Emily Dickinson said over a hundred years ago, "Narcotics cannot still the Tooth / That nibbles at the soul." Because this is my presupposition I find it less than magnificent that Christianity, arriving a little late on the biblical scene, should take eternal life so completely for granted and should find it both obvious and inevitable that the confession of Jesus as Lord or the belief that Christ is with God would have to be explicated within the theology of general resurrection else Christian faith might be in vain. My further presupposition is that the future of Christian theology will demand of us a God who does not grant one eternal life to remedy an earth beyond divine control, and who did not grant Christ resurrection in posthumous vindication of some prehumous abandonment. There are and will be other ways of confessing Jesus as Lord and other theologies of how Christ is with God.

My concern in this is a conviction that only by a full and glad acceptance of our utter finitude can we experience authentic transcendence. Immortality, no matter how carefully qualified as divine gratuity, strikes me as a genuflection before our own hope, a worship of our own imagination. To quote one final time from Helmuth Plessner on time and death. "But his having laid bare his own finiteness means a confrontation with it, which limits it for him, which makes it questionable and fragmentary. The knowledge of his finiteness reveals the contrary possibility, and now in a sense other than the survival discernible in the reproduction that compensates for the death of the individual." The choice that I see confronting us is between transcendence and immortality, and given that choice I find only one selection possible.

Jesus and Apocalyptic

I wish to examine three sayings of Jesus which together offer a radical and comic revision of dominant themes in apocalyptic expectation. These sayings have been described by Norman Perrin as "three crucial sayings . . . for the authenticity of which it is possible to offer strong arguments, and they present the fundamental emphases of the teachings of Jesus concerning the Kingdom." Their combination, then, is not just at my own prejudice.

Individual not National: In Luke 11:20, and also Matt 12:28, Jesus claimed, "But if it is by the finger of God that I cast out demons, then the kingdom of God has come upon you." Instead of God's kingdom coming in catastrophic vengeance on the forces of evil and in eternal reward for the just, there is *only* the curing of a possessed person. Instead of the cosmic ending of the whole world there is only the individual ending of one human being's world of demonic anguish. And that, Jesus asserts, is eschatology; that is the coming of God. It is the radical reversal of human world and not the destruction of the material globe. But it should also be noted that in the Greek text the final "has come upon *you*" is plural not singular. To one but for all.

Present not Future: The second saying is found in Luke 17:20–21 where it is carefully explained by Luke's addition of the succeeding 17:22–24. "Being asked by the Pharisees when the kingdom of God was coming, he answered them, 'The kingdom of God is not coming with signs to be observed; nor will they say, "Lo, here it is!" or "There!" for behold, the kingdom of God is in the midst of you.'" The Greek phrase translated as "in the midst of you" could also be taken to mean "within you" in a spatial/spiritual sense rather than in the temporal/historical sense accepted here. Such a spiritual reading in which the kingdom of God is hidden within the secrecy of the individual soul has a long and honorable ancestry going all the way back to this gloss in Thom 3: "Jesus said: If those who lead you say to you: 'See, the Kingdom is in heaven', then the birds of the heaven will precede you. If they say to you: 'It is in the sea', then fish will precede you. But the Kingdom is within you and it is without you." The much more likely interpretation for Jesus' meaning is that the kingdom is not a future entity for which one may await prevenient signs but is a reality already among the hearers. Indeed, it is to this sense that two other versions of the saying in that same Gospel of Thomas seem to point. In Thom 51, "His disciples said to Him: When will the repose of the dead come about and when will the new world come? He said to them: What you expect has come, but you know it not." And in Thom 113, "His disciples said to Him: When will the Kingdom come? [Jesus said:] It will not come by expectation; they will not say: 'See, here', or: 'See, there'. But the Kingdom of the Father is spread upon the earth and men do not see it." The distinction is not between inside and outside (whatever that really means), but between something which, being future, might be watched for with human eyes, and something which is already and always present but needs faith to be recognized. Once again a commentary from Emily Dickinson is helpful:

> Not Revelation—'tis—that waits,
> But our unfurnished eyes—

Suffering not Triumphant: In some ways this third saying may be the most radical of them all. It appears in Matt 11:12, "From the days of John the Baptist until now, the kingdom of heaven has suffered violence, and men of violence take it by force." There is another version in Luke 16:16, but it has been heavily edited. "The law and the prophets were until John;

since then the good news of the kingdom of God is preached, and every one enters it violently." For Luke the violence is the severe spiritual asceticism and even physical persecution through which the individual forces passage into the kingdom. But the viewpoint in Matthew is far different. Here the kingdom is not a triumphant apocalyptic force before which all evil and injustice must fall so that the just may be vindicated for their suffering. Rather has the kingdom itself become subject to opposition and even to the possibility of destruction and the saying gives us no assurance that it will ever be otherwise.

Over against an apocalyptic kingdom of God which is cosmic, future, and triumphant, Jesus announces one which starts with the individual but is open thence to all, which is present already but only to faith, and which is assured of continual opposition rather than secure and ultimate victory. Rilke: "Who talks of victory? To endure is all."

Borges on Immortality

One might certainly debate whether Jesus' total rejection of the apocalyptic imagination entails a similar prophetic denial of any form of eternal life for the individual. I would argue that it does but I also recognize the problem in separating his authentic teaching from that of the early church which placed on his lips so much of its own later faith in resurrection and immortality. The Pharisees believed strongly in the general resurrection. And it may well be that here, as in so many other cases, Jesus was in severe disagreement with their theology.

With Borges, at least, the position is clear. Robert Anderson has quoted his comment that, "Time is a tremulous and exigent problem of metaphysics; eternity is a game, a worn-out hope." And Arthur Natella has found that "Borges uses grey as a symbol of eternity (since it is vague and indefinite), and it is frequently the only descriptive color he uses to describe his immortal characters." It is also not exactly a cheerful or hopeful color.

The narrator of Borges's 1970 story "The Duel" remarks that, "My suspicion is that in Heaven the Blessed are of the opinion that the advantages of that locale have been overrated by theologians who were never actually there. Perhaps even in Hell the damned are not always satisfied." And Borges himself, in that New York University interview cited a few times before, admits that, "I don't want to be threatened by personal immortality of any kind. I only think of an afterlife as a kind of awful possibility, but I think we should rather speak of it as a kind of awful *im*possibility."

Finally, and especially, there are the two similarly entitled stories, "The Immortal" from 1947 and "The Immortals" in 1966.

"The Immortal" opens with a description of the fortuitous discovery of a certain manuscript and closes with a discussion of its authenticity. In the main part of the story an Author-I cedes place to a Narrator-I whose life extended from being Marcus Flaminius Rufus, tribune under Diocletian, to being the antique dealer Joseph Cartaphilus of Smyrna who died in 1929. The tribune had discovered the City of the Immortals and drunk from the waters of immortality. The City "abounded in dead-end corridors, high unattainable windows, portentous doors which led to a cell or pit, incredible inverted stairways whose steps and balustrades hung downwards." And the Immortals did not live in it but dwelt in nearby caves and looked like troglydites. Immortality had bored them back to savagery and silence. He teaches one to speak and finds that he is Homer, but in immortality there is no real individuality, and Rufus himself had spoken Homeric Greek after he drank the waters of immortality. Centuries later, as Cartaphilus, he comes ashore near a certain port (Footnote by Author: "There is an erasure in the manuscript; perhaps the name of the port has been removed"). "On the outskirts of the city I saw a spring of clear water; I tasted it, prompted by habit. When I came up the bank, a spiny bush lacerated the back of my hand. The unusual pain seemed very acute to me. Incredulous, speechless and happy, I contemplated the precious formation of a slow drop of blood. Once again I am mortal, I repeated to myself, once again I am like all men. That night, I slept until dawn . . ." Mortality, with its pain and with its sleep, is preferred to an immortality which makes both language and individuality superfluous.

The second story, "The Immortals," is a much simpler tale of a doctor who has perfected a technique so that one can live forever as cubes in his laboratory. "The brain, refreshed night and day by a system of electrical charges, is the last organic bulwark in which ball bearings and cells collaborate. The rest is Formica, steel, plastics. Respiration, alimentation, generation, mobility—elimination itself!—belong to the past. . . . Oral declaration, dialogue, may still be improved." The price for such immortality is, once again, language. And for Borges the price is too high. In his own comments on this terribly contemporary story Borges has said that, "In 'The Immortals' we are face to face with people who are only immortal and nothing else, and the prospect, I trust, is appalling."

I am reminded once again of Schmendrick the Magician in *The Last Unicorn* for whom language is more precious than immortality as it is also for Borges. "But he knew what they meant, and he knew exactly how to say them, and he knew that he could say them again when he wanted to, in the same way or in a different way. Now he spoke them gently and with joy, and as he did so he felt his immortality fall away from him like armor, or like a shroud."

4. Plot

I have discussed Borges's fascination with circular time both as a comic critique of linear or biblical time, and also as a labyrinth of play plotted into many of his stories. Before comparing some time/theme similarities in both Jesus and Borges, I want to study in detail the vision of time which Jesus plotted into one short but devastating parable, a story which just barely qualifies for Aristotle's definition of plot as requiring a beginning, a middle, and an end.

The Hidden Treasure

The story of "The Hidden Treasure" is so short that it can be given in full rather than in synopsis. "The kingdom of heaven is like treasure hidden in a field, which a man found and covered up; then in his joy he goes and sells all that he has and buys that field."

I wish to compare Jesus' story with two other stories on the same theme taken from rabbinical literature to hear how his version might have sounded to his contemporaries. This is on the principle advocated by M. A. K. Halliday that, "a text is meaningful not only in virtue of what it is but also in virtue of what it might have been. The most relevant exponent of the 'might have been' of a work of literature is another work of literature."

Here then are two slightly different versions of that story from the Rabbis. In *Midrash Rabbah* on the biblical Song of Songs there is this version of the story. ". . . like a man who inherited a piece of ground used as a dunghill. Being an indolent man, he went and sold it for a trifling sum. The purchaser began working and digging it up, and he found a treasure there, out of which he built himself a fine palace, and he began going about in public followed by a retinue of servants—all out of the treasure he found in it. When the seller saw it he was ready to choke, and he exclaimed, 'Alas, what have I thrown away.'" A second version has been translated by J. D. Kingsbury as follows:

To what is the matter like? To one who received a large field in a province of the sea [i.e. in the far distance, in the remote West] as inheritance. And he sold it for a trifle. And the buyer went there and dug it up and found in it treasures of silver and treasures of gold and precious stones and pearls. Then the seller began to choke himself [for anger.] This is what the Egyptians did; for they sent away and did not know what they sent away; for it is written, "And they said: What is this we have done, that we have let Israel go from serving us?" (Exodus 14.5).

Before comparing the poetics of these three stories, one from Jesus and two from the Rabbis, I shall introduce two further principles which specify the one from Halliday already quoted. First, from Roman Jakobson: "The reader of a poem or the viewer of a painting has a vivid awareness of two orders: the traditional canon and the artistic novelty as a deviation from that canon." So we must watch for hidden polemic in Jesus' story vis-à-vis the established authority of rabbinical versions. Second, from John Lyons: "the *less* probable a particular element is, the *more* meaning it has in that context ('element' should here be taken to refer to all the results of 'choice', including silence, permitted by the system of communication for particular contexts.)" We must also watch, then, for the polemics of the unexpected.

The first rabbinical story represents a moral *example* which castigates laziness and extols hard work. It has a balanced negative and positive moral. There is a version of the story also in Thom 109 which has a very similar function although the negative seems more emphasized in this case. The second rabbinical story is a historical *allegory* for Exodus 14:5. Notice how the treasure has been adapted to match 12:35 where the Israelites "asked of the Egyptians jewelry of silver and of gold" and received it in booty before departing Egypt.

But apart from these interpretive emphases it is immediately obvious that the rabbinical stories are much closer to one another than either is to the version of Jesus. There are two major differences between the Rabbis and Jesus. First, they record the activity of both the Seller and the Buyer so that the former's activity (sells . . . fumes) frames that of the latter. Second, and more important, the rabbinical Buyer traverses this sequence: *Buys, Acts (ploughs), Finds*; but Jesus' Buyer proceeds in exactly the opposite direction: *Finds, Acts (sells), Buys*. Put more simply: finding precedes buying for Jesus but buying precedes finding for the Rabbis. I would note in passing that Jesus' sequence makes the action of the Buyer if not illegal at least slightly immoral. It is not exactly what one would boast of having done except in carefully chosen company. Third, and most important, there is a very different sense of time behind that simple reversal of the main verbs, buying/finding. The time of the rabbinical stories leads logically and almost inevitably from Past to Present to Future. Its linear temporality shows the sweep from laziness and loss, through work-ethic and discovery, and projects into the future with the palace and the retinue in the forefront and the fuming seller in the background. For Jesus this linear time is broken so that the sequence is Future to Past to Present. Out of his unknown and unexpected Future comes the treasure's opportunity. For it he gladly abandons his entire Past by selling all his possessions. And thereby he obtains field, treasure, and a new Present. *And at this point Jesus stops.* The new Present remains unspecified in his story and we almost want to ask: Then what happened? But Jesus concludes with the Present of the treasure's enjoyment and, of course, there always looms the possibility of a new Future to start the play all over again. Linear time is no longer something which has a set and closed past, a sure and secure present, and a relatively known and projected future. But neither is it changed into circular time. It bespeaks instead the ascendancy of the future as advent over a past which it can reverse and reinterpret at any moment and on which a present which means also a gift can now be built.

Other Stories, Other Treasures

The comparison of Jesus' story with that of the Rabbis was not intended to exalt one over the other but to differentiate their functions as clearly as possible. Jesus' story is a parable, the paradox of time formed into story. Their stories were moral example (this is what you should or should not do) and historical allegory (this is what the Israelites and the Egyptians did).

This can be developed by glancing at a few other variations on the theme of hidden treasure from other sources. It is of crucial importance in these cases, as also between Jesus and the Rabbis, to notice the major choices which bring the story out this way rather than that. One can imagine a map of narrative possibilities within the general theme of hidden treasure and then focus on the crossroads where major decisions have been made. W. H. Gass has emphasized this in his *Fiction and the Figures of Life.* "The story must be told and its telling is a record of the choices, inadvertent or deliberate, the author made from all the possibilities of language," and, of course, the labyrinthine novel of Ts'ui Pên had exemplified it in "The Garden of Forking Paths" by Borges: "In all fictional works, each time a man is confronted with several alternatives, he chooses one and eliminates the others; in the fiction of Ts'ui Pên, he chooses—simultaneously—all of them. *He creates*, in this way, diverse futures, diverse times which themselves also proliferate and fork." Ts'ui Pên's novel *The Garden of Forking Paths* from Borges's story of the same name and Herbert Quain's novel *April March* from Borges's story "An Examination of the Work of Herbert Quain" have the same intention of simultaneous narrative cartography. But while the former novel works forward the latter one proceeds backward attempting various reconstructions which might all lead to the same conclusion. Together the two novels are a structuralist dream or possibly even a semiological nightmare.

Three modern examples, then, of stories of hidden treasure remembering, to coin a phrase, that where your treasure is there your heart is also. First, Gerald T. Hurley wrote an article on "Buried Treasure Tales in America" for *Western Folklore* in 1951 in which he claimed that the characteristic sequence of such stories is Hiding, Seeking, NOT Finding. "American treasure tales usually end with the treasure *not* being found." This point is stated at the start and repeated at the end of the article: "Is it recovered? In American buried treasure tales the answer is, with very few exceptions, *no*." I leave to your imagination some rather obvious explanations for this absence against the background of the American workethic.

Second, T. Roszak in *Where the Wasteland Ends* tells this story. "Over many generations a people busy themselves hiding a treasure. They become obsessed with the devising of safeguards, pitfalls, snares, barriers. Finally, the treasure is ingeniously sequestered, but so well that not even the people themselves can find it . . . nor can they any longer remember what it was they hid. *And then*, there arises a generation which begins to doubt that there ever was a treasure in the first place! So they ask, 'Were our ancestors not perhaps badly mistaken about the existence of these riches?' "

Third, beyond both American pragmatism and European nihilism, I would tell the story myself as I hear it at present. I do so as a variation on the epigraph Elie Wiesel used for *The Gates of the Forest* and I hope the adaptation will not be deemed irreverent.

When the great Rabbi Israel Baal Shem-Tov saw destitution threatening the Jews it was his custom to go into a certain part of the forest to meditate. There he would light a fire, say a special prayer, a hidden treasure would be revealed, and destitution averted. Later, when his disciple, the celebrated Magid of Mezritch, had occasion, for the same reason, to intercede with heaven, he would go to the same place in the forest and say: "Master of the Universe, listen! I do not know how to light the fire, but I am still able to say the prayer." And again the hidden treasure would be revealed. Still later, Rabbi Moshe-Leib of Sasor, in order to save his people once more, would go into the forest and say: "I do not know how to light the fire, I do not know the prayer, but I know the place and this must be sufficient." It was sufficient and the hidden treasure was revealed. Then it fell to Rabbi Israel of Rizhyn to overcome misfortune. Sitting in his armchair, his head in his hands, he spoke to God: "I am unable to light the fire and I do not know the prayer; I cannot even find the place in the forest. All I can do is to tell the story, and this must be sufficient." And it was sufficient.

The hidden treasure in the story is the story of the hidden treasure.

Time and Theme

This temporality of Jesus in which future as advent changes the interpretation of the past and grounds the present as gift appears again in his stories of "The Pearl Merchant" and "The Great Fish." In the former "the kingdom of heaven is like a merchant in search of fine pearls, who, on *finding* one pearl of great value, went and *sold* all that he had, and *bought* it." My italics indicate its similarity to the structure of "The Hidden Treasure."

"The Great Fish" can also be given in full but in the version from the Gospel of Thomas. "The Man is like a wise fisherman who cast his net into the sea, he drew it up from the sea full of small fish; among them he *found* a large and good fish, that wise fisherman, he *threw* all the small fish down into the sea, he *chose* the large fish without regret." Once again my italics indicate the structure. This version in Thomas is radically changed in Matthew so that the sequence of time in Jesus' story (found-threw-chose) is no longer evident. In Matthew the fisherman simply divides good fish from bad on the shore and so also will the angels at the end of the world.

Apart from these three parables where the paradoxical reversal of past-present-future into future-past-present is strongly underlined, most of the parables of Jesus place a temporal emphasis either on the gratuitous and fortuitous nature of the future as advent, or on the radical revision of past interpretive security which such an advent entails, or on the challenge of the new and open present which must now be faced.

Future as Advent: Themes such as search and/or surprise emphasize this aspect of future not as something planned, projected, and expected, but as something totally unexpected or radically adventitious. Examples would be the contrast between harvest plenitude and sowing losses seen already in "The Sower" or the similar paradoxical contrast of tiny beginning and final pastoral serenity in "The Mustard Seed." The invisibility of presence but the visibility of effect is seen in "The Leaven" and "The Budding Fig Tree." And the joy of the search's success dominates both "The Lost Sheep" and "The Lost Coin."

Similar themes of search and surprise have been noted by James E. Irby in many of Borges's stories and with very similar result. "The chance discovery or event, which apparently has no cause, is like a tangential contact between two greatly diverse planes of existence, an intrusion or interpolation whose origin lies 'beyond.'" Borges himself has tried to move from surprise as surprise ending to a more total one which permeates the entire story. In an interview in Buenos Aires in May of 1960 he said, "If there is to be astonishment, I prefer that it be complete; I have renounced partial and bordered surprises." And in the 1970 Preface to *Doctor Brodie's Report* he repeated, "I have given up the surprises inherent in a baroque style as well as the surprises that lead to an unforeseen ending." I take both these assertions with large grains of salt. Borgesian surprise was far more often total rather than terminal. He has never read like O. Henry or Agatha Christie for reasons that L. A. Murillo has indicated most clearly. "The reader becomes involved in Borges's stories as he cannot become involved in the solution of a detective mystery or a chess problem or a theorem of higher mathematics because the conjecture is about radical questions of human existence, time, personal will, consciousness, and destiny." With Jesus and with Borges surprise is always more total than terminal, more in the telling than just in the ending of the story.

Past as Reversal: I have already indicated in the Third Variation a number of Jesus' stories where, metonymically or metaphorically, secure interpretations of the past as the fixed basis for a fixed present were thrown into polar reversal. Once again Irby has found a similar phenomenon in many of Borges's stories. "All these movements culminate, if not in death, in some kind of ironic reversal or submission, in terms of which purely individual desires, ambitions and goals in the realm of immediate reality are shown to be illusory and the individual is subordinated to a higher order."

For Jesus, as for the prophets, this means that God is Lord of the past not because our memory can be changed but because our imagination can be challenged. The Exodus from Egypt could not and would not ever be the same event once the Babylonian Exile had taken place. Borges has not envisioned this relativity of the past as fully as might have been expected, possibly because of the allure of circular time which gives the past much more than its due. In "New Refutation of Time" he claimed that, "Neither vengeance nor pardon nor prisons nor even oblivion can modify the invulnerable past." Possibly they cannot, but any act of imagination strong enough to stir the human soul can turn this invulnerable past quite inside out. This is the peculiar weakness of his 1948 story "The Other Death." In his own commentary on the story he derives its genesis from the fact that, "All theologians have denied God one miracle—that of undoing the past." In the story Pedro Damián died a coward's death at the battle of Masoller, but God answers his final prayer and slowly but surely memories are changed until his commanding officer can remember only his bravery, "So fearless, and barely twenty." This is one way to handle the past but it is a somewhat uneconomic way. Jesus suggests a far simpler one: a new treasure begets a changed past.

Present as Action: There are a whole set of stories by Jesus whose most striking element is not the content of the story itself *but his failure to give any interpretation of them or application to them.* They are images of challenge and they describe how individuals either fail or succeed or both when confronted with situations demanding decisive action.

Once again a comparison with a rabbinical story may clarify the point. Joachim Jeremias has drawn attention to the story told by one Rabbi at the funeral of another who had died at an early age. A king hired laborers and, inspecting them after two hours of work, he detached one from the group and walked up and down talking with him until evening. And at evening all received the same wages so that some protested. The king answered: "I have not wronged you; this laborer has done more in two hours than you have done during the whole day." The funeral oration ended by applying the story to the early death of the Rabbi. Here everything is solved and the application of the story is perfectly clear. But what is most unnerving about similar stories from Jesus is their *total lack of explanation or application.* They combine an absolute challenge to action with a complete silence on what action is to be undertaken in real life.

Compare, for example, the above rabbinical tale with Jesus' similar story of "The Vineyard Workers." In this story all the workers receive equal pay and the pay is just and fair but it is also totally unexpected since the workers have been hired at various stages of the day's progress. And absolutely no explanation is given so that Matt 20:15 feels constrained to add that the master did it out of goodness which will hardly convince anyone who considers that *goodness and generosity*, if that were the point, might easily have been established by the master paying *everyone alike three times the promised amount.* Jesus' story is not about goodness but about surprise. The master is not one who is generous but one who acts unexpectedly and protest is our ordinary human reaction to the unexpected.

(It may be noted in passing that this phenomenon of unspecified or unexplicated demand strikes a chord in our contemporary consciousness. R. E. Olderman in *Beyond the Waste Land* has said that, "The call to action remains a workable theme only so long as the author resists telling us what that action should be. Once again, the symbolic affirmation that transcends conflicts without offering a program of action is just about the only affirmative ending the novel of the sixties can have without running into sociology or romanticism.")

Those stories which I referred to in my book *In Parables* as parables of action all have this surprising absence of application, and this would have struck original hearers attuned to rabbinical stories as both disturbing and even paradoxical. The tradition has, of course, supplied applications to many of them in and by their present evangelical contexts but the interpretive diversity serves only to underline the original absence of any interpretation given officially by Jesus himself. For example, Jesus has many parables involving a master and servant in which the latter must act decisively for fear of punishment or at least reprimand. But, time after time, we are admonished to act wisely, prudently, decisively, but are never told what such action means or entails. Jesus does not specify because such application is our own personal fate and our own individual destiny. It will always depend on what treasure it has been given us to find.

There is one interesting comparison between this type of story with Jesus and a similar type in Borges. There is a startling amount of violence in Borges's stories. Think, for example, of how two gauchos consummate "The End of the Duel" by racing against one another for a few strides *after* their throats had been slit. Or, how the two brothers in "The Intruder" solved their problem by killing the woman who had come between them. Finally, there is the awful efficiency and chilling determination with which "Emma Zunz" gives herself to a random sailor in preparation for killing her employer, pleading self-defense after "rape," and thereby avenging her father's death.

The tradition was early dismayed by the fact that some of Jesus' stories invoked images of lethal if prudential efficiency, of murderous violence which precluded quite obviously any usage of such stories as moral examples. The most famous of such stories is "The Evil Tenants." We have already seen what the tradition had to do to make this story acceptable. Another example, in honor of Borges's fascination with the knife, is a story by Jesus which has left no trace in the canonical literature but is found only in Thomas. Many scholars, however, are convinced that it is quite authentic and originally from Jesus. It is "The Assassin" and is very short and very reminiscent of contemporary Zealot politics against the Romans in Palestine. "The Kingdom of the Father is like a man who wishes to kill a powerful man. He drew the sword in his house, he stuck it into the wall, in order to know whether his hand would carry through; then he slew the powerful man." Recall Ronald Christ's apt if awful phrase on Borges using "the criminal as artist."

Together, these stories, from Jesus and from Borges, challenge us to a different and more creative sense of time, to something like that suggested by Frank Kermode in *The Sense of an Ending*. "The *kairos* arrives, the moment when at last the time is free, by means of a divine *peripeteia*, by accidental judgments and purposes mistook; we cannot make ready for it simply by 'taking the long view.' And when it comes it is an end, in so far as human affairs have ends. It is not a universal end, merely an image of it."

Fifth Variation:
Person and Persona

> A man sets himself the task of portraying the world. Through the years he peoples a space with images of provinces, kingdoms, mountains, bays, ships, islands, fishes, rooms, instruments, stars, horses, and people. Shortly before his death, he discovers that that patient labyrinth of lines traces the image of his face.
>
> Jorge Luis Borges

Comparisons of genre and theme lead to this final Variation which contrasts the persona of Jesus and of Borges. A note on that epigraph. Does it mean that an artist's total creativity *copies* the artist's personality or that it *creates* the artistic persona?

1. PERSONA

What I mean by the term persona can be indicated best in conjunction with terms such as intention and personality.

Intention and Personality

In his book *Validity in Interpretation* E. D. Hirsch claimed that, "Verbal meaning is whatever someone has *willed* to convey by a particular sequence of linguistic signs and which *can* be conveyed (shared) by means of those linguistic signs." Notice the duality indicated by my italics. This same basic dichotomy haunts the entire book. *Commentary* involves a double activity. It includes both *understanding* which derives from *interpretation* of *meaning*, that is, the meaning intended by the original author. But it also includes *judgment* which stems from *criticism* of *significance*, that is, the significance accepted by the contemporary reader. Granted this dichotomy, Hirsch will accept hierarchy: "*Criticism* is, by its nature, more valuable than *interpretation* alone, particularly when it is *criticism* which embraces *interpretation*" (my italics again for the technical terms). This establishment of commentary's validity on the objective rock of authorial intention is open to at least three major objections. First, authorial intention cannot be checked where and when it is most needed save by accepting the debates of historians instead of the arguments of literary critics. Second, even if the author is neither dead nor anonymous, the explanation is itself in language and so needs another one *ad infinitum*. Third, it is not at all clear how one gets from *meaning* to *significance* even if one could establish the former by authorial intention and yet Hirsch has conceded that this combination is more important than either *meaning* or *significance* taken alone.

A way out of this impasse has been indicated by Dorothea Krook who proposed that, "The distinction directly relevant to literary criticism is that between the *author's* intention and the *work's* intention." She called the former intention "authorial or subjective" and the latter one "enacted or objective." It is possible to distinguish authorial intention into subconscious, unconscious, and conscious, and, while all of this is legitimate material for study, it needs the psychologist rather than the literary critic. It is the enacted, objective intentionality of the work which is the domain of the literary critic precisely as such. And this intention is known, judged, and interpreted against the manifold possibilities of language. It is best to leave the first half ("willed") of Hirsch's definition to the psychologist and to rest content with the second part as the challenge of literary criticism: what "can be conveyed (shared) by means of those linguistic signs."

But even if we ignore authorial intention how can one ignore authorial personality? Surely it is the personality that holds a corpus of work together and makes it possible, say, to speak of a Jesus and a Borges.

It is well known, of course, that authorial personality, the

Person of the Author, was ushered out peremptorily by T. S. Eliot's famous essay on "Tradition and the Individual Talent" with its dictum that the, "poet has, not a 'personality' to express but a particular medium." And in his story *The Birthplace* Henry James had Morris Gedge assert that, " 'The play's the thing.' Let the author alone." A few lines later, even more firmly, "There *is* no such Person" as the author. The objection, "But wasn't *there*—?" is stifled at birth by his stern and even violent insistence. "There was somebody. But They've killed Him. And, dead as He is, They keep it up, They do it over again, They kill Him every day."

I want, therefore, to leave aside completely both authorial intention and authorial personality. I recognize the special difficulty of authors who create an "artistic personality" for public display apart from but alongside their creative work. In such cases this personality is itself a creative invention. Boris Tomashevsky recognized this problem fifty years ago and insisted that,

What the literary historian really needs is the biographical legend created by the author himself. Only such a legend is a *literary fact*. As far as "documentary biographies" are concerned, these belong to the domain of cultural history, on a par with the biographies of generals and inventors. With regard to literature and its history, these biographies may be considered only as external (even if necessary) reference material of an auxiliary nature.

Even more interesting is what Heinz Politzer has claimed in the case of Kafka. Instead of Kafka having gone from authorial personality into the "I" of his letters and diaries and so into the characters of his stories, it may be that he went in the opposite direction. "It is more than probable that he even shaped the 'I' which expresses itself in his letters and diaries after the model of the heroes in his books—one more reason to be careful in the use of this biographical material for the interpretation of his literary writings. Instead of lifting the material of his books out of the shapeless mass of his life experiences, he may well have lived his life as if it were one of his writings." In another sense, then, his letters, his diaries, and his stories are but different literary forms for the same literary creativity. Personality is disappearing into persona.

Not, then, the author's intention but the work's intention, and not the personality but the persona is of present interest. I do not really want to ask either Jesus or Borges what they intended by this or that story, even had I the chance,

> Lest Interview—annul a want—
> That Image—satisfies—

as Emily Dickinson knew long, long ago. (And she also knew how to be a poetic persona in her letters just as much as Kafka.)

By persona I understand the accumulated and total construct of an author as literary creator. I intend that unity of corpus which would be discerned between certain works in any adequate poetics even if they had been scattered anonymously across time and place like autumn leaves in an autumn wind. Unity of persona does not derive from unity of personality but from a coherence and a concentration discernible in the works themselves.

It is only fair to admit that I am not at all sure there is a personality behind or apart from persona. I am inclined to think that what we recognize most clearly in the artist is true of all of us in less spectacular ways. Persona may well be what we all are. We are the coherence of what we creatively present to one another. So I end with thoughts similar to these of Ronald Christ on Borges, "Perhaps it will seem that I'm playing with (and failing at) biography, thematics, or worse still, psychology. That's a risk I'll have to take, relying all the while on you to keep in mind that the image, the *persona*, the 'naked mask' is what I want to see, what I think needs to be seen, and not the man or the mind or the spirit behind the mask, *if indeed we can still believe in such things.*" My italics at the end.

Revelation's Imminence

Before considering the persona of Borges and of Jesus separately I wish to indicate the point where both visions come most forcibly together. Comic eschatology has been the general motif for this conjunction throughout the book. This might also be specified as the *permanence of revelation's imminence.*

First, Borges. His 1950 essay "The Wall and the Books" closed with this haunting evocation of revelation's permanent imminence. "Music, states of happiness, mythology, faces belabored by time, certain twilights and certain places try to tell us something, or have said something we should not have missed, or are about to say something; this imminence of a revelation which does not occur is, perhaps, the aesthetic phenomenon." This reappears later in two of his stories. "The End," written in 1952-53, locates the possibility in place and time. "There is an hour of the afternoon when the plain is on the verge of saying something. It never says it, or perhaps it says it infinitely, or perhaps we do not understand it, or we understand it and it is as untranslatable as music." And in 1969 the story of "Pedro Salvadores" rephrases the theme once again. "As with so many things, the fate of Pedro Salvadores strikes us as a symbol of something we are about to understand, but never quite do."

In commenting on this theory the American critic Carter Wheelock has said that, "The 'imminence of a revelation' is perhaps the ultimate knowable reality, and men do not create it. They comprise it, behold it, and try to transmute it into language. This idea precludes any esthetic theory—that is, any rule or formula for producing an imminent revelation." One wishes to agree and disagree at the same time. Yes, if we are talking of mechanical effects that produce an imminent revelation as coins do Cokes. No, if we are talking about, for example, "Pedro Salvadores" itself. Borges opened this story with a promise, "To meddle as little as possible in the telling, to abstain from picturesque details or personal conjectures." But by the time he, Borges, has told us the story we accept that closing comment cited earlier and hardly notice the ironic contradiction with the story's deferential opening which had promised us an impersonal narration. We have been brought to a point of imminent revelation by this story and this is precisely what such stories are intended to do to us. They force us out to the borders of languuge and the limits of story and at such points revelation is permanently possible. This is how the French critic Gérard Genette has understood Borges's point. "The meaning of books is in front of them and not behind them; it is in us: a book is not a ready-made meaning, a revelation we have to suffer; it is a reservation of forms that are waiting to have some meaning, it is the 'imminence of a revelation that is not yet produced,' and that every one of us has to produce for himself."

It is here the Borges's *permanently imminent revelation* and Jesus' *kingdom of God* intersect with one another. The stories of Jesus are not allegories which tell the hearer what God is like or how God acts upon the world. Neither are they moral examples which give the audience practical models of good conduct to be followed or practical cases of evil action to be avoided. They are parables whose metaphorical or metonymical paradoxes break open the closed security of the hearer's world and in that comic eschatology make possible the revelatory experience which is permanently imminent.

In his poem "John 1:14" Borges has God say this of Borges:

I have entrusted the writing of these words to a common man;
they will never be what I want to say
but only their shadow.
These signs are dropped from My eternity.

Jesus was satisfied to tell a certain kind of story and say only that God's advent, God's kingdom, was like that. Borges tells his tales and hints only of imminent but ever absent revelation. But both alike understand and accept the sufficiency of signs and shadows where any more would be too little.

2. BORGES

Borges himself has commented on the distinction of personality and persona by proposing a disjunction between Borges and *Borges*. Borges suggested this distinction unless, of course, it was *Borges* who did it.

Borges and *Borges*

His best-known commentary on the problem is "Borges and Myself," also translated as "Borges and I." He has termed it "this all-too-famous sketch" and it has been anthologized in four different collections of his works. But I wish to start with an even earlier rendition of this theme of individual personality versus authorial persona.

In the special Borges number of *Modern Fiction Studies* Donald A. Yates has an article entitled "Behind 'Borges and I,'" and the following is taken from this short but fascinating study.

For nine years between 1937 and 1946 Borges "was given a job as second assistant in a dingy municipal library in the shabby lower middle-class worker's district of Almagro" in Buenos Aires. His fellow workers had no idea who he was and even when they found his name in an encyclopedia they dismissed it as an interesting coincidence and no more. Borges was a librarian, *Borges* was a writer. Yates discovered in the same workbook in which "Tlön, Uqbar, Orbis Tertius" had been composed a half page of prose dating from 1940. The piece is entitled simply "Jorge Luis Borges." It records in precise and clinical detail the suicide of a certain second assistant librarian identified as "The other J. L. B. (the other and real Borges, the one who justifies me in a sufficient and secret way)." And the suicide "left behind this poem, evidently written down at the library (as the letterhead shows), which I copy textually." The poem was never included in the original workbook and, although Yates "discovered" it in another workbook, it had never been finished. (Borges could not remember the poem or what happened to it. Neither could *Borges*.)

For myself I am much more impressed by the poem's original absence than by its present discovery. And I am inclined much less than Yates to consider the prose piece as a failed first draft for the later "Borges and Myself." It can stand quite brilliantly and even devastatingly by itself—and preferably without any poem included. In it, as it now stands, *Borges* the writer murders Borges the librarian by suicide. But it is Borges who writes the suicide poem! Borges has become totally destroyed and absorbed into *Borges*. There could be no poem of Borges appended to the story.

In 1956, sixteen years later, he wrote "Borges and Myself." This single-page work contrasts the Person-I with the Persona-Borges, the I which walks around Buenos Aires with the Borges who writes "his tales and poems." In my terms Person-I is Borges and Persona-Borges is simply *Borges*. But: "Little by little, I have been surrendering everything to him, even though I have evidence of his stubborn habit of falsification and exaggeration. . . . And so, my life is a running away, and I lose everything and everything is left to oblivion or to the other man." The only major difference between this and the 1940 version is that now *Borges* is absorbing Borges slowly and steadily rather than absorbing him in the instant of a suicide. But then comes the conclusion which forces the *reader* personally into the dilemma: "Which of us is writing this page I don't know." If the writer is now totally and exclusively *Borges*, who is the reader?

Borges as *Borges*

Even apart from those two writings critics have always been aware of how *Borges* quite deliberately fashions Borges into *Borges*. And others record it as fact without realizing its magnificent and most appropriate irony. M. S. Stabb has said that "talking with Borges is a 'confirmation' of what one deduces about the man from his books rather than a revelation of a 'different' Borges." Borges is just like *Borges*. How amazing!

Ronald Christ, however, is quite clear about *Borges's* tampering with what is residually intractable in Borges. "Borges is creating his own biography here, choosing what events and circumstances he will allow, in his writing, to be responsible for his authorial personality." The most interesting example is *Borges's* insistence that it was a near-fatal illness in 1939 which turned him to writing those *ficciones* which were to make him famous. "The birth of an idiosyncratic narrative from the matrix of hallucination, high fever, and near death; a birth assisted by a literary fantasy which ironically verifies comprehensible reality" is, as Christ has pointed out, exceedingly appropriate. But, as we saw earlier, "The Approach to Al-Mu'tasim" dates from 1935 and had already been slipped into the 1936 volume *Historia de la eternidad*. All of which means that the persona of *Borges* still needs some retelling and rewriting. Once again, from Ronald Christ: "Borges arranges the separation of his authorial and personal selves—that is, he labors at the creation of an author for this work. That author, the man who has not lived but written and read (Borges doesn't tire of repeating it), that author whom we name when we say 'Borges'—that author is the character Borges has created, a character whose *Life* is the *obras completas* of Jorge Luis Borges." Borges is *Borges*.

Borges and Comic Eschatology

Fifty years ago Borges could already claim with a certain youthful brashness that, "I have already overcome my poverty; I have recognized, among thousands, the nine or ten words that accord with my heart. I have already written more than one book in order to be able to write, perhaps, a single page. The justifying page, which may be an abbreviation of my destiny." What is this page, this persona, Borges in *Borges*?

Richard Howard's poem "Prose for Borges" prefaced the special issue of *TriQuarterly* bearing the same title and it summed up Borges with these lines:

> The cancellings, the negations are never
>   ultimate, are never one last wipe
>   that clears the lens, a farewell
>   to supersession, finale of ruin.

His persona does not evoke any definitive and final eschatology, not cosmic but rather comic eschatology, and therefore this:

>   A language not out to
>   eliminate itself, resolute rather
>
> to make a stay, creating the boundaries
>   it strikes against.

This eschatology moves us beyond both apocalyptic bang and nihilistic whimper by inviting us to play in and with the play of world.

Carter Wheelock's book *The Mythmaker* repeatedly focuses on "Borges's world-dissolution," on this Borges who "breaks up the world intellectually, who negates intellectually any particular utopia or eschatological goal." What is the strategy of this comic eschatology? "Borges plays with his reader and knows that most of his fictions constitute puzzles that attack the mind at its most vulnerable spot: the imperious hunger for the explanation of it all." If the reader allows Borges to have his way then "fiction, art, imagination—all involve the abandonment of one's fixed world and a movement into another, and this movement involves, however briefly, a return to myth (chaos)." But it is precisely the willingness for this most dangerous passage that founds and grounds our humanity because "out of that pregnancy some more adequate God, some better language may come, though it be faceless and wordless."

Comic eschatology sends us out repeatedly into that chaos where alone we can encounter a God who is not just our own projected vanity.

3. Jesus

With Borges I was able to discuss his own explicit commentary on the problem of individual personality and authorial persona and to indicate the final absorption of the former by the latter. With Jesus, of course, there is no such direct discussion but the problem has also much more interesting theological ramifications for the future of Christian thought. So my procedure here will have to be indirect.

Jesus, Christ and Lord

Primitive Christianity believed that the risen Jesus was enthroned in triumph at the right hand of God whence he would eventually return in apocalyptic judgment to punish evil and to reward the elect. In such a faith it is no surprise that the Risen Lord himself should speak in ecstatic admonition or prophetic message on the lips of Christian teachers. Paul will continually invoke this authority in writing letters to his churches and John could announce the vision in Revelation 2:13 of "one like a son of man, clothed with a long robe and with a golden girdle round his breast." It would be no surprise at all if interest was focused totally on the present and the future rather than on the past, if one talked of Heaven but not of Galilee. *Letters* and *Apocalypses* are forms we would have expected but the startling novelty is *Gospels*, works which combine past, present, and future so that the Palestinian past of Jesus' life is totally interwoven with the present situation of the writer's community and the full hope and expectation of that community is retrojected as promises onto the lips of the Galilean Jesus. In his recent book *The New Testament: An Introduction*, Norman Perrin summed this up by saying that "they created a whole tradition portraying him already in his earthly ministry as exercising the authority that would be his when he came as Son of Man." Since they were much more concerned with professing their own faith and building up their own communities than with transmitting clear and distinct documentation for modern historians, they combined data "based partly on actual reminiscences of his ministry and teaching, partly on experience of him in the present, and partly on an expectation of him in the future. But in all this the *form* was the form of sayings and stories of Jesus in what we would call his earthly ministry." In a word, earthly Jesus and Heavenly Lord are completely interwoven so that Jesus speaks to a woman at a Samaritan well but the message is intended by John 4 for his own community at a very different time and in a very different place. In all this it is the person of Jesus as the Christ, the Risen Lord, whose present heavenly authority is guiding his community on earth. Against such a background any search for the actual historical Jesus might seem hopeless at best and presumptuous at worst.

The Historical Jesus

How is it possible to decide from our present gospel texts what actually comes from Jesus since around seventy years of tradition has been selectively retrojected onto his lips? How did I decide throughout this book what came from Jesus and what belongs to Christ? I am asking what *method* is adequate to this type of *material*. If one disagrees on the nature of the material, of the documents, by claiming, for example, that the Gospels are eyewitness biographies, this would have to be discussed before any questions of methodology could be profitably raised.

Any criteria for the historical authenticity of sayings or stories must work their way through four narrowing circles of general problematic. There is, first, the ambiguity, uncertainty, and insecurity of any and all historical research. Second, there is the difficulty that all this happened long ago and in another country, and besides they all are dead. Third, there is the nature of our sources which are, quite openly and honestly, confessional witness rather than uncommitted chronicle. Fourth, there is the problem of constant adaptation, application, and interpretation which offers us multiple versions of the same unit within successive or even simultaneous layers of the tradition.

It is, in fact, the last problem that brings with it the best avenue of solution, if solution be at all possible. If, and only if, one agrees that creative reinterpretation for renewed relevance is the constant in our data and if one can chart the trajectory of such readaptation and reapplication, one could see what was there originally in need of all this reinterpretation. This is why the *criterion of dissimilarity* must be the basic criterion for authenticity in historical Jesus research. This criterion or principle proposes that the most likely authentic material coming from Jesus will appear where there is divergence from or dissimilarity with the emphases of the primitive community which both transmitted and transformed such materials. The principle is logically persuasive *only* if one has decided that creative change is what strikes one most forcibly in any careful reading of our texts. Indeed, in many cases, one discovers that the material is being changed back into greater harmony with certain emphases in contemporary Judaism by the early church. Any other criteria, such as multiple attestation or content similarity, must be secondary to and dependent on this basic criterion of dissimilarity. It should also be stressed that dissimilarity does not of itself claim superiority—let alone uniqueness—for Jesus. Any such claims would have to be vindicated by what one finds through this criterion, but they are not the presupposition which created it.

I have accepted throughout this book the criterion of dissimilarity as a necessary and negative discipline imposed by the nature of the materials themselves. But with one very important qualification. I applied it, first and foremost, to *form* rather than to *content*. What forms of language and modes of speech did Jesus use which were dissimilar to those forms used by the primitive church and which this tradition tried valiantly to change into greater harmony with the standard and expected forms of contemporary Judaism. Even a priori one would expect that forms might endure even with multiple changes of content within them.

You will recall how constantly and consistently I argued in this book that the *forms* of Jesus' language were being slowly but surely changed back into the *forms* of language already known from and in Judaic tradition. Case parody was becoming case law, antibeatitude beatitude, paradox proverb, and parables were being interpreted and then changed into moral examples and/or historical allegories. And it is precisely their *formal* resistance to all such *formal* mutation that draws our present attention to these elements and isolates them as belonging with some critical security to the historical Jesus himself.

From this I do not conclude that the Jesus of history and the Christ of faith have no continuity with one another. (The Jesus of history was also a challenge to faith, by the way.) But the continuity can no longer be glibly established by saying, on the one hand, that Jesus is the presupposition of Christianity, or, on the other, that Christianity is implicit in Jesus. Continuity can be found, however, where the parabler becomes the Parable, where Jesus who spoke in paradoxes becomes acknowledged as the Paradox of God. But that means, of course, that the continuity is in language and not in heaven.

Jesus and Comic Eschatology

When I speak of Jesus I am not thinking of a personality once existent in Palestine and now in continued personal existence in heaven. By Jesus I intend the persona of Jesus, that is the vision and the challenge of the language of Jesus. At one time the search for the historical Jesus was interested in his self-consciousness or his self-understanding. In the Preface to my own book *In Parables* I said that I was not "concerned with the psychological self-consciousness or even the theological self-understanding of Jesus" but with "the language of Jesus." I am no longer certain what that distinction means and an inclined now to equate consciousness and language. It is not so much a question of Jesus' persona against his personality but rather the absorption of personality into persona and of person into language. Were I to put this now against past Christian theology I would question whether the Lordship of Jesus derives from the permanence of his personality in heaven or from the continuance of his persona in language.

What, then, is the persona of Jesus? It is the extension of the Mosaic iconoclasm into language itself. The God of Israel cannot be portrayed in images of wood and stone, silver and gold, but neither can God be trapped in forms of law and wisdom, prophecy and apocalyptic. The content of Jesus' language is an attack on form within all the major tradition's of Israel's inheritance. Such content is intrinsically eschatological, forcing world and language to its knees before the aniconic God of Israel. But, yet, *against* language only *in, with, and by* language. And therefore, comic. Which is something we are not quite ready to hear.

Was there no iconoclastic laughter in Palestine at the time of Jesus? When Mikhail Bakhtin ended his marvelous study of Rabelais by saying, "We repeat, every act of world history was accompanied by a laughing chorus," should he have made an explicit exception for Judaism and for Jesus? I find it much more plausible that Jesus knew and spoke from out the comic irony which dictates that only *in* language is language conquered, only *by* language is language humbled, and only *from* language is language transcended.

When I think of Jesus, then, it is not anything said by anyone in the New Testament which comes most immediately to my mind. I have to borrow words which Emily Dickinson originally applied to a very different subject. "The brow is that of Deity—the eyes, those of the lost, but the power lies in the *throat*—pleading, sovereign, savage—the panther and the dove!"

4. ORPHEUS

In John Updike's 1965 article for *The New Yorker* he talked of Borges's "ecumenic and problematic and unconsoling theology." He said that "while Christianity is not dead in Borges, it *sleeps* in him, and its dreams are fitful." He concluded that "Borges is a pre-Christian."

The theology of Jesus is equally ecumenic, problematic, and unconsoling, and he too is a pre-Christian. Indeed, it is a very great pity that Judaism gave him up so easily to Christianity. It is a great pity for Christianity. Whether it is also one for Judaism is not for me to say.

Since Jesus and Borges are both pre-Christians I shall conclude by bringing them both under the aegis of a vision certainly older than Christianity and possibly even wiser. Emily Dickinson once more: "Orpheus' Sermon captivated— / It did not condemn—"

Lyre and Voice

The first element of an Orphic vision is that Apollo's bard does not sing without accompanying himself on the lyre. Lyre and voice together yet the lyre was there before the voice began and will still be there when the song is over. *The Orphic lyre is language itself*, and it is with this and on this medium the Orphic song is sung.

Take, for example, this statement from Carter Wheelock's book on Borges which I cited frequently earlier in this final

Variation. "Men are doomed to possess their world as language which cannot bespeak the objective order but can only reflect the imperfect memories of the mind." Three immediate objections. First, why "doomed"? Why our doom and not our glory? What player feels doomed by the laws and exigencies of a favorite game? Would you have it otherwise and what would that otherwise look like? We are the music while the music lasts. Second, what is this "objective order" and where did it come from and how do we know it exists? What is outside language is silence and chaos (so named in language), and they are infinitely precious and absolutely necessary as sea to boat but what mariner plans to leave the boat and walk on the waters? There is no objective order except language itself. Third, and as correlative, "only" and "imperfect" are meaningless terms since no alternative is possible. This *is* the way, this *is* the perfect.

Compare, then, this statement concerning language from another article on Borges, this time by William H. Gass. "We may indeed suspect that the real power of historical events lies in their descriptions; only by virtue of their passage into language can they continue to occur, and once recorded (even if no more than as gossip), they become peculiarly atemporal." The lyre of language is not our doom but our destiny. Our songs are always sung to the lyre and this lyre we must always play for ourselves.

Play and Death

This second element is just as important as the preceding one. The point I wish to stress is that the song of the bard cannot help him to avoid his own death or to prevent the death of the one he loves. And maybe that is far too negative a way of putting it. Recall T. S. Eliot's essay once again. "The progress of an artist is a continual self-sacrifice, a continual extinction of personality." The personality must go if the persona is to remain or, better, the personality dies so that we understand the persona alone was there all along. The Orphic song perdures.

Compare, then, Books 10 and 11 of Ovid's *Metamorphoses*.

First, the death of the beloved and the song of the bard are placed in juxtaposition. Book 10 records the story of Orpheus and Eurydice which is probably the best-known section of the entire myth. For example, Walter A. Strauss wrote a book in 1971 called *Descent and Return*, subtitled "The Orphic Theme in Modern Literature." Eurydice dies and Orpheus descends after her to plead for her release from Hades. "As he spoke thus, accompanying his words with the music of his lyre, the bloodless spirits wept." But, as we know so well, he looked back at her before reaching the upper earth and thus lost her once more to death.

The bard cannot save his beloved from death but he can sing and create thereby a place of refuge. "A hill there was, and on the hill a wide-extending plain, green with luxuriant grass; but the place was devoid of shade. When here the heaven-descended bard sat down and smote his sounding lyre, shade came to the place." And so also came the trees, the birds, and the animals. "Such was the grove the bard had drawn, and he sat, the central figure in an assembly of wild beasts and birds. And when he had tried the chords by touching them with his thumb, and his ears told him that the notes were in harmony although they were of different pitch, he raised his voice in this song." The bard who cannot save his beloved Eurydice from death can establish on earth a place of shade and bring all of nature's wildness into harmonious peace with his lyre and with his voice.

Second, the bard's own death is contrasted with his song's continuance. Book 11 offers a climactic development of this theme of play and death. The life and the song of Orpheus are such as infuriate the Maenads ("See, see the man who scorns us!"), and they attack him even "While with such songs the bard of Thrace drew the trees, held beasts enthralled and constrained stones to follow him." Their own howlings must first drown out the Orphic song since their weapons are "harmless under the spell of song . . . and then at last the stones were reddened with the blood of the bard whose voice they could not hear." They not only killed him, they tore him to pieces with "hoes, long mattocks and heavy grubbing-tools." But then: "The poet's limbs lay scattered all around; but his head and lyre, O Hebrus, thou didst receive, and (a marvel!) while they floated in mid-stream the lyre gave forth some mournful notes, mournfully the lifeless lips murmured, mournfully the banks replied." It is this section of the myth, lesser known than the Eurydice incident, which gave the title to an even more important 1971 book by Ihab Hassan, *The Dismemberment of Orpheus* subtitled "Toward a Postmodern Literature."

The Orphic song cannot save Orpheus himself from death and dismemberment, but still the lyre is struck and still the voice is heard. Orpheus goes but the Orphic song remains. So Hassan quotes Rilke's line in the "Sonnets to Orpheus" saying, "He has to vanish, so you'll understand." The person of Orpheus dies but the Orphic persona remains.

Orpheus cannot save from death either Eurydice or himself, but past such death the Orphic lyre remains and so does the Orphic voice. As Borges said of "Plain Things,"

> Past our oblivion they will live on,
> familiar, blind, not knowing we have gone.

Or Emily Dickinson, with this:

> A word left careless on a page
> May consecrate an eye
> When folded in perpetual seam
> The wrinkled author lie.

And even more succinctly, with this: "The Poets light but Lamps— / Themselves—go out—." Still more important is the possibility that song arrives not despite but because of death. From her letters: "And so I sing, as the Boy does by the Burying Ground—because I am afraid," or, "I myself, in my smaller way, sang off charnel steps."

Song cannot conquer death but then neither can death conquer song. The singer must go but not necessarily the song. As with all our play there must be and always is a time limit. Perhaps that is both necessary and enough.

Notes

The numbers at the left refer to the pages of this book. A work will be fully cited when first noted. Any later citations will be abbreviated.

Page
ii T. S. Eliot, "East Coker," *Four Quartets* (New York: Harcourt, Brace & World, 1943), pp. 30–31.
vii J. L. Borges, "An Autobiographical Essay," *Aleph*, p. 138.
xiii P. S. Beagle, *The Last Unicorn* (New York: Ballantine, 1969), p. 4.
xiv F. Jameson, *The Prison-House of Language* (Princeton, N.J.: Princeton U. Press, 1972), p. vii.
T. S. Kuhn, *The Structure of Scientific Revolutions* (2nd ed.; Chicago: U. of C. Press, 1970), p. 85.
xv P. Ricoeur, "The Problem of the Double-Sense as Hermeneutic Problem and as Semantic Problem," *Myths and Symbols*, ed. J. M. Kitagawa and C. H. Long (Chicago: U. of C. Press, 1969), pp. 63–79 (see 79).
3 F. Kafka, *The Great Wall of China* (New York: Schocken, 1960), p. 284.
R. Barthes, *Mythologies* (New York: Hill & Wang, 1972). The first two quotes terminate the introductions to the 1957 and 1970 French editions. The third quote is from his *Critical Essays* (Evanston, Ill.: Northwestern U. Press, 1972), pp. 177–78.
G. Poulet, as cited by J. Hillis Miller, "The Geneva School," *Critical Quarterly* 8 (1966): 305–21 (see 315–16).
J. Barth, "The Literature of Exhaustion," *Atlantic Monthly* 220, no. 2 (August 1967): 29–34 (see 32).

Page

4 E. M. Cioran, *The Temptation to Exist*, trans. R. Howard (Chicago: Quadrangle Books, 1968), p. 146.

S. Sontag, "The Aesthetics of Silence," *Styles of Radical Will* (New York: Farrar, Straus & Giroux, 1969), pp. 3–34 (see 4).

J. Peterkiewicz, *The Other Side of Silence* (New York: Oxford U. Press, 1970), p. 126.

5 A. R. Ammons, "A Poem is a Walk," *Epoch* 18 (Fall 1968): 114–119 (see 119).

9 J. L. Borges, "The Analytical Language of John Wilkins," *OI*, pp. 101–105.

F. Nietzsche, "The Joyful Wisdom," *The Complete Works of Friedrich Nietzsche* (New York: Russell & Russell, 1964), vol. 10, p. 32.

11 E. Welsford, *The Fool: His Social and Literary History* (New York: Farrar & Rinehart, 1935). See pp. 52 and 320.

R. B. Martin, "Notes toward a Comic Fiction," *The Theory of the Novel: New Essays*, ed. J. Halperin (New York: Oxford U. Press, 1974), pp. 71–90 (see 73).

12 Plato, *The Republic*, trans. B. Jowett (New York: Modern Library, n.d.), pp. 360, 364–68.

Aristotle, *Aristotle's Rhetoric and Poetics*, trans. I. Bywater (New York: Modern Library, 1954), pp. 225, 227, 229.

A. Cameron, *The Identity of Oedipus the King* (New York: N.Y.U. Press, 1968), p. xvi.

13 E. S. Rabkin, *Narrative Suspense* (Ann Arbor, Mich: U. of Michigan Press, 1973), pp. 151–52.

14 H. Bergson, "Laughter," *Comedy*, ed. Wylie Sypher (Garden City, N.Y.: Doubleday, 1956), pp. 63–64.

15 J.-P. Vernant, "Greek Tragedy: Problems of Interpretation," *The Languages of Criticism and the Sciences of Man*, ed. R. Macksey and E. Donato (Baltimore, Md.: Johns Hopkins Press, 1970), pp. 273–89 (see 281).

16 Plato, *Lysis-Symposium-Gorgias*, trans. W. R. M. Lamb (New York: Putnam, 1932), pp. 243–44.

R. B. Martin, *Notes toward a Comic Fiction*, p. 79.

Page

17 C. Fry, "Comedy," *Comedy: Meaning and Form*, ed. R. W. Corrigan (Scranton, Penn.: Chandler, 1965), pp. 15–17.
W. Sypher, "The Meanings of Comedy," *Comedy*, p. 195.

18 A. Robbe-Grillet, as cited by J. Peterkiewicz, *The Other Side of Silence*, p. 66.
W. Sypher, *Comedy*, pp. 201 and 212 respectively.
N. Frye, *Anatomy of Criticism* (New York: Atheneum, 1970), p. 178.
A. Koestler, "The Comic," *Insight and Outlook* (Lincoln, Neb.: U. of Nebraska Press, 1949), pp. 1–110 (see 75 and 83).

19 M. Bakhtin, *Rabelais and His World* (Cambridge, Mass.: MIT Press, 1968), p. 51.
W. Sypher, *Comedy*, pp. 254, 252, 206 respectively.
W. H. Auden, "Notes on the Comic," *The Dyer's Hand* (New York: Random House, 1952), pp. 371–85 (see 371).

20 O. Wilde, as cited in R. B. Martin, *Notes Toward a Comic Fiction*, p. 84.
K. Vonnegut, Jr., *Cat's Cradle* (New York: Dell, 1963), pp. 111–12.

21 N. A. Scott, Jr., "The Bias of Comedy and the Narrow Escape into Faith," *The Christian Faith* 44 (1961): 9–39 = *Comedy: Meaning and Form*, pp. 81–115 = *The Broken Center* (New Haven, Conn.: Yale U. Press, 1966), pp. 77–118.
F. M. Cornford, *The Origin of Attic Comedy* (London: Cambridge U. Press, 1934 [^{1}1914]), pp. vii, 3, 190–220.

22 W. Sypher, *Comedy*, p. 220.

25 J. Huizinga, *Homo Ludens* (Boston: Beacon Press, 1955). See pp. 13 and 173.

26 J. Ehrmann, "Homo Ludens Revisited," *Game, Play, Literature* = *Yale French Studies* 41 (1968): 31–57 (see 33–34, 56).

27 E. Fink, *Oase des Glücks: Gedanken zu einer Ontologie des Spiels* (Freiburg: Karl Alber Verlag, 1957). Translated ex-

Page

cerpts (with some overlaps) have appeared as "The Ontology of Play," *Philosophy Today* 4 (1960): 95–110 = 18 (1974): 147–61; and "The oasis of happiness: Toward an ontology of play," *Game, Play, Literature* = *Yale French Studies* 41 (1968): 19–30. My quotations are from *PhilT* 18 (1974): 160, 161.

28   J. Huizinga, *Homo Ludens*, p. 92.
Plato, *Laws*, trans. R. G. Bury, Loeb Classical Library, 2 vols. (New York: Putnam, 1926), vol. 2, p. 55.

30   W. B. Yeats, "The Tower," *The Collected Poems of W. B. Yeats* (def. ed.; New York: Macmillan, 1956), p. 196; *Autobiographies* (New York: Macmillan, 1927), p. 430.

31   W. Sypher, *Comedy*, pp. 207, 208.

32   S. Beckett, *Watt* (New York: Grove Press, 1959), p. 48.
S. Cavell, "Ending the Waiting Game," *Must We Mean What We Say?* (New York: Scribners, 1969), pp. 115–62 (see 149).

33   M. C. Swabey, *Comic Laughter: A Philosophical Essay* (New Haven, Conn.: Yale U. Press, 1961), p. 17.
W. Sypher, *Comedy*, p. 237.
J. Piaget, *Structuralism* (New York: Basic Books, 1970), p. 5.

34   J. Derrida, "Structure, Sign, and Play in the Discourse of the Human Sciences," *The Languages of Criticism*, pp. 247–72 (see 260).
G. Crespy, "De la structure à l'analyse structurale," *Etudes Théologiques et Religieuses* 48 (1973): 11–34.

35   K. Vonnegut, Jr., *Breakfast of Champions* (New York: Delta, 1973), p. 241.
V. Turner, *The Ritual Process* (Chicago: Aldine, 1969), pp. 109–13, 128, 169, 176–78, 185, 191.

37   M. Bakhtin, *Rabelais and His World*, pp. 6, 9, 11.

38   F. de Saussure, *Course in General Linguistics* (New York: McGraw-Hill, 1966), pp. 22–23, 88–89, 110 (for chess); 16 (for semiology).

Page

39 E. Benveniste, as cited by L. Bersani, "Is There a Science of Literature?," *Partisan Review* 39 (1972): 535–53 (see 536).
R. Barthes, "Elements of Semiology," *Writing Degree Zero and Elements of Semiology* (Boston: Beacon, 1967), p. 11.
R. Scholes, *Structuralism in Literature: An Introduction* (New Haven, Conn.: Yale U. Press, 1974), p. 16.
R. Barthes, *Critical Essays*, p. 160.

40 R. Barthes, *On Racine* (New York: Hill & Wang, 1964), p. ix.
V. Shklovsky, "Art as Technique," *Russian Formalist Criticism* (Lincoln, Neb.: U. of Nebraska Press, 1965), pp. 5–24 (see 12–13).
V. Erlich, *Russian Formalism: History—Doctrine* (The Hague: Mouton, 1965), p. 176.

41 B. Tomashevsky, "Thematics," *Russian Formalist Criticism*, pp. 62–95 (see 66–67).
M. Sternberg, "What is Exposition? An Essay in Temporal Delimitation," *The Theory of the Novel*, pp. 25–70 (see 35).

42 T. S. Eliot, "Tradition and the Individual Talent," *Selected Essays* (new ed.; New York: Harcourt, Brace & World, 1950), pp. 3–11 [from 1919].
T. Todorov, *The Fantastic* (Cleveland: Case Western Reserve University Press, 1973), p. 6.

43 R. A. Lanham, *Style: An Anti-Textbook* (New Haven, Conn.: Yale U. Press, 1974), pp. 10–11, 47.
J. L. Borges, as cited by Anna María Barrenechea, *Borges the Labyrinth Maker* (New York: N.Y.U. Press, 1965), p. 81.
R. Otto, *The Idea of the Holy* (London: Oxford U. Press, 1923).

45 D. E. Turner, *Borge's Game with Shifting Mirrors*, Ph.D. dissertation, University of Texas at Austin (Ann Arbor, Mich.: University Microfilms, 1970), p. 206.
K. Vonnegut, Jr., *Cat's Cradle*, p. 177; *The Sirens of Titan* (New York: Dell, 1959), pp. 297, 301.

46 C. Hyers, *Zen and the Comic Spirit* (Philadelphia: Westminster, 1973), pp. 15, 103.

Page

47   S. Kierkegaard, *Concluding Unscientific Postscript*, trans. D. F. Swenson and W. Lowrie (Princeton, N.J.: Princeton U. Press, 1941), pp. 448, 413 resp.

49   S. Sontag, *Styles of Radical Will*, pp. 21–22.

50   E. Rodríguez-Monegal, "Symbols in Borges' Work," *MFSBN*, pp. 325–40 (see 332).

L. Harss and B. Dohmann, "Jorge Luis Borges, or the Consolation by Philosophy," *Into the Mainstream* (New York: Harper & Row, 1966), pp. 102–36 (see 129).

J. R. Ayora, *A Study of Time in the Essays and Short Stories of Jorge Luis Borges* Ph.D. dissertation, Vanderbilt University (Ann Arbor, Mich.: University Microfilms, 1969), p. 220.

J. Peterkiewicz, *The Other Side of Silence: The Poet at the Limits of Language* (New York: Oxford U. Press, 1970).

R. M. Rilke, *Selected Works: II. Poetry*, trans. J. B. Leishman (New York: New Directions, 1967), p. 257.

R. J. Christ, *The Narrow Act: Borges' Art of Allusion* (New York: N.Y.U. Press, 1969), pp. 155–56, 190.

51   J. E. Irby, *The Structure of the Stories of Jorge Luis Borges*, Ph.D. dissertation, U. of Michigan (Ann Arbor, Mich.: University Microfilms, 1962), p. 199, note 20.

C. Wheelock, *The Mythmaker: A Study of Motif and Symbol in the Short Stories of Jorge Luis Borges* (Austin: U. of Texas, 1969), p. 50.

53   F. W. Weber, "Borges's Stories: Fiction and Philosophy," *Hispanic Review* 36 (1968): 124–41 (see 125–26, 141).

55   J. L. Borges, as cited, respectively, in R. Christ, *The Narrow Act*, p. 36; and in K. Botsford, "About Borges and Not About Borges," *Kenyon Review* 26 (1964): 723–37 (see 729).

58   O. Eissfeldt, *The Old Testament* (New York: Harper & Row, 1965), p. 479.

61   H. Bloom, *The Anxiety of Influence* (New York: Oxford U. Press, 1973).

Page

M. Krieger, "Mediation, Language, and Vision in Literature," *Interpretation: Theory and Practice*, ed. C. S. Singleton (Baltimore, Md.: Johns Hopkins Press, 1969), pp. 211–42 (see 226, 229.)

62 C. Guillén, *Literature as System* (Princeton, N.J.: Princeton U. Press, 1971), pp. 121, 128.

A. Fowler, "The Life and Death of Literary Forms," *New Literary History* 2 (1970–1): 199–216.

63 V. Shklovsky, "Sterne's *Tristram Shandy*: Stylistic Commentary," *Russian Formalist Criticism*, pp. 27–57 (see 27, 57).

65 A. Olrik, "Epic Laws of Folk Narrative," *The Study of Folklore*, ed. A. Dundes (Englewood Cliffs, N.J.: Prentice-Hall, 1965), pp. 129–41 (see 134). Original dates to 1909.

68 A. Camus, "Return to Tipasa," (1952) *The Myth of Sisyphus and Other Essays* (New York: Knopf, 1967), p. 203.

M. Heidegger, "Letter on Humanism," *Philosophy in the Twentieth Century*, ed., W. Barrett and H. Auden (New York: Random House, 1962), pp. 270–302. See also R. H. Cousineau, *Heidegger, Humanism and Ethics* (Louvain: Editions Nauwelaerts, 1972).

69 A. Jolles, as summarized in R. Scholes, *Structuralism in Literature*, pp. 45–46.

72 W. A. Beardslee, "The Wisdom Tradition and the Synoptic Gospels," *Journal of the American Academy of Religion* 35 (1967): 231–40; *Literary Criticism of the New Testament* (Philadelphia: Fortress, 1970), pp. 30–41; "Uses of the Proverb in the Synoptic Gospels," *Interpretation* 24 (1970): 61–76; "Proverbs in the Gospel of Thomas," *Studies in New Testament and Early Christian Literature: Essays for A. P. Wikgren*, ed. D. E. Aune; NovTSup 33 (Leiden: Brill, 1972), pp. 92–103. My quotations are from "Thomas," p. 103 and "Uses," p. 67, respectively.

73 E. Pound, *The Cantos of Ezra Pound* (New York: New Directions, 1972), pp. 795–96 and 511 respectively.

Page

75 W. Sypher, *Comedy*, p. 233.

77 E. Dickinson, *The Letters of Emily Dickinson*, ed. T. H. Johnson, 3 vols. (Cambridge, Mass.: The Belknap Press of Harvard U. Press, 1958), vol. 3, p. 691 (#690).

78 L. Harss and B. Dohmann, *Into the Mainstream*, p. 121.
    T. E. Lyon, "Borges and the (Somewhat) Personal Narrator," *MFSBN* 363–72 (see 367).

79 A. Reid, "Borges as Reader," *PFB* 100–101.

81 J. Stark, "Borges' 'Tlön, Uqbar, Orbis Tertius' and Nabokov's *Pale Fire*: Literature of Exhaustion," *Texas Studies in Literature and Language* 14 (Spring 1972): 139–45 (see 140, 142).
    W. Stevens, "Another Weeping Woman," *The Collected Poems of Wallace Stevens* (New York: Knopf, 1954), p. 25.

83 M. D'Lugo, "Binary Vision in the Borgian Narrative," *Romance Notes* 13 (1972): 425–431 (see 425, 431).

84 R. Scholes, *Elements of Fiction* (London: Oxford U. Press, 1968), pp. 78–88 (see 84).

88 R. Burgin, *Conversations with Jorge Luis Borges* (New York: Holt, Rinehart & Winston, 1968), pp. 58–59.
    R. Christ, *The Narrow Act*, p. 6.

89 S. Sosnowski, "'The God's Script'—A Kabbalistic Quest," *MFSBN* 381–94 (see 381).
    F. W. Weber, "Borges's Stories," p. 140.

91 J. Updike, "The Author as Librarian," *The New Yorker*, October 30, 1965, pp. 223–46 (see 245).
    D. E. Turner, *Borges' Game*, p. 206.
    W. K. Wimsatt and M. C. Beardsley, "The Intentional Fallacy," *Sewanee Review* 54 (1946): 468–88; "The Affective Fallacy," *SR* 57 (1949): 31–55 = W. K. Wimsatt, *The Verbal Icon* (Lexington: U. of Kentucky Press, 1954), pp. 3–18, 21–39.
    T. Todorov, *The Fantastic*, pp. 167 and 120 respectively.

Notes

Page
92 R. M. Rilke, *Poems 1906 to 1926*, trans. J. B. Leishman (New York: New Directions, 1957), p. 222.
The Poetry of Robert Frost, ed. E. C. Lathem (New York: Holt, Rinehart & Winston, 1969), p. 260.

93 J. L. Borges, *DBR* x.
H. Politzer, "Franz Kafka and Albert Camus: Parables for Our Time," *Chicago Review* 14, no. 1 (Spring 1960): 47–67 (see 63); *Franz Kafka: Parable and Paradox* (Ithaca, N.Y.: Cornell U. Press, 1962); rev. & expanded, 1966, pp. 84–85.

94 E. Dickinson, *The Poems of Emily Dickinson*, ed. T. H. Johnson, 3 vols. (Boston: The Belknap Press of Harvard U. Press, 1955), vol. 2, p. 771 (#1095).

96 J. Miles, "Laughing at the Bible: Jonah as Parody," *The Jewish Quarterly Review* 65 (1975): 168–81.

98 R. M. Rilke, *Poems*, p. 239.
C. Lévi-Strauss, "The Structural Study of Myth," *Structural Anthropology* (Garden City, N.Y.: Doubleday, 1967), pp. 202–28 (see 226).
E. Leach, *Genesis as Myth and Other Essays*, Cape Editions, 39 (London: Cape, 1969), p. 11.
P. Maranda, ed., *Mythology* (Baltimore, Md.: Penguin, 1972), p. 213.

99 V. Turner, *The Ritual Process* (Chicago: Aldine, 1969); *Dramas, Fields, and Metaphors* (Ithaca, N.Y.: Cornell U. Press, 1974).
W. B. Yeats, "The Tower," p. 287.

102 P. Ricoeur, "The Socius and the Neighbor," *History and Truth* (Evanston, Ill.: Northwestern U. Press, 1965), pp. 98–109.
R. Barthes, "Introduction à l'analyse structurale des récits," *Communications* 8 (1966): 1–27 (see 19).
T. Todorov, *The Fantastic*, p. 31.

Page

104 L. Tolstoy, "What Men Live By," *Twenty-Three Tales* (New York: Oxford University Press, 1971), pp. 55–82.

105 H. Fielding, *Joseph Andrews*, ed. M. C. Battestin (Middletown, Conn.: Wesleyan U. Press, 1967), pp. 51–57.

107 R. Jakobson and M. Halle, *Fundamentals of Language*, Janua Linguarum, NR 1 ('S-Gravenhage: Mouton, 1956), pp. 52–82 (see 76–77).

109 J. Jeremias, *The Parables of Jesus*, (rev. ed.; New York: Scribners, 1963), p. 183.

113 J. L. Borges, "Borges at N.Y.U.," ed. R. Christ, *PFB* 444–59 (see 446).
H. Politzer, *Parable and Paradox*, pp. 63 and 352 respectively.

114 J. E. Irby, *The Structure*, pp. 47, 286, 54 respectively.
B. Belitt, "The enigmatic predicament: some parables of Kafka and Borges," *PFB* 268–293 (see 270, 272–73).

115 J. D. Crossan, *In Parables: The Challenge of the Historical Jesus* (New York: Harper & Row, 1973). See also, since this book, "Structuralist Analysis and the Parables of Jesus," *Semeia* 1 (1974): 192–221; "The Good Samaritan: Towards a Generic Definition of Parable," *Semeia* 2 (1974): 82–112, 121–28; and *The Dark Interval: Towards a Theology of Story* (Chicago: Argus Communications, 1975).

116 N. Hawthorne, *Hawthorne's Short Stories* (New York: Knopf, 1964), pp. 399–410 (see 410).
R. Scholes and R. Kellogg, *The Nature of Narrative* (New York: Oxford U. Press, 1966), pp. 106–7.

117 Paul de Man, "The Rhetoric of Temporality," *Interpretation: Theory and Practice*, p. 194.

118 R. Lima, interview in Buenos Aires, 23 May 1960, cited in his "Notes by the Editor" to A. M. Barrenechea, *Borges the Labyrinth Maker*, p. 151.
A. M. Barrenechea, *Borges the Labyrinth Maker*.
R. Christ, *The Narrow Act*.

Notes

Page
119 C. Wheelock, "Borges' New Prose," *PFB* 403–440 (see 408).
     A. Fletcher, *Allegory: The Theory of a Symbolic Mode* (Ithaca, N.Y.: Cornell U. Press, 1964), pp. 22 and 238.
120 M. Murrin, *The Veil of Allegory* (Chicago: U. of C. Press, 1969), pp. 9, 22–23, 168.
121 E. Honig, *Dark Conceit: The Making of Allegory* (Cambridge, Mass.: Walker-de Berry, 1960), p. 12.
122 M. Abrams, as cited in Paul de Man, "The Rhetoric of Temporality," p. 179.
     H. James, as cited in E. Honig, *Dark Conceit*, p. 52.
123 R. Coover, *Pricksongs and Descants* (New York: New American Library, 1969), p. 78.
     H. Politzer, *Parable and Paradox*, pp. 1–22.
125 P. S. Beagle, *The Last Unicorn*, pp. 1 and 6.
126 M. Bakhtin, *Rabelais and His World*, p. 123.
127 R. Barthes, "Style and Its Image," *Literary Style: A Symposium*, ed. S. Chatman (New York: Oxford U. Press, 1971), pp. 1–15 (see 10).
130 E. Honig, *Dark Conceit*, p. 5.
131 B. Brecht, as cited by A. Fletcher, *Allegory: The Theory*, p. 82.
133 J. L. Borges, "New Refutation of Time," *Lab* 234 = *PA* 64 = *OI* 187.
135 *Man and Time*, Papers from the Eranos Yearbooks, ed. J. Campbell, Bollingen Series 30, vol. 3 (New York: Pantheon, 1957). Citations from H.-C. Puech (pp. 39–40), H. Plessner (pp. 245–46), and G. van der Leeuw (pp. 329, 338–39, 350).
138 P. S. Beagle, *The Last Unicorn*, p. 108.
     J. L. Borges, *Borges at N.Y.U.*, pp. 448–49.
140 A. M. Barrenechea, *Borges*, p. 16.
141 J. R. Ayora, *A Study of Time*, pp. 218 and 103 respectively.
     R. Christ, *The Narrow Act*, p. 20.

Page
142 A. M. Barrenechea, *Borges the Labyrinth Maker*, p. 111.
     J. Alazraki, *Jorge Luis Borges*, Columbia Essays on Modern Writers 57 (New York: Columbia U. Press, 1971), p. 36.
     L. M. Hinman, "Nietzsche's Philosophy of Play," *Philosophy Today* 18 (1974): 106–24. See also *The Portable Nietzsche*, ed. and trans. W. Kaufmann (New York: Viking, 1954), pp. 137–40.

144 L. A. Murillo, "The Labyrinths of Jorge Luis Borges: An Introduction to the Stories of *The Aleph*," *Modern Language Quarterly* 20 (1959): 259–66 (see 266).
     H. E. Lewald, "The Labyrinth of Time and Place in Two Stories by Borges," *Hispania* 45 (1962): 630–36 (see 631).
     N. D. Isaacs, "The Labyrinth of Art in Four Ficciones of Jorge Luis Borges," *Studies in Short Fiction* 6 (1968–9): 383–94 (see 385, 386).

145 G. Quispel, "Time and History in Patristic Christianity," *Man and Time*, pp. 85–107 (see 94).

147 "Book of the Dead," *Ancient Near Eastern Texts Relating to the Old Testament*, ed. J. B. Pritchard (2nd ed.; Princeton, N.J.: Princeton U. Press, 1955), pp. 34–36.

148 *The Poetry of Robert Frost*, p. 386.
     E. Dickinson, *The Poems*, vol. 2, p. 385 (#501).

183 H. Plessner, *Man and Time*, pp. 245–46.

149 N. Perrin, *Rediscovering the Teaching of Jesus* (New York: Harper & Row, 1967), p. 63.

150 E. Dickinson, *The Letters*, vol. 2, p. 424 (#280) = *The Poems*, vol. 2, p. 530 (#685).

151 R. M. Rilke, "For Wolf Graf von Kalckreuth," *Selected Works*, p. 210.
     R. R. Anderson, "Jorge Luis Borges and the Circle of Time," *Revista de Estudios hispánicos* 3 (1969): 313–18 (see 317).
     A. A. Natella, Jr., "Symbolic Grey in the Stories of Jorge Luis Borges," *Romance Notes* 14 (1972): 258–61 (see 258).

152 J. L. Borges, *Borges at N.Y.U.*, p. 450.

Notes

Page
153 P. S. Beagle, *The Last Unicorn*, p. 219.
154 M. A. K. Halliday, "The Linguistic Study of Literary Texts," *Proceedings of the Ninth International Congress of Linguists, 1962*, ed. H. A. Lunt, Janua Linguarum: Series Maior, 12 (The Hague: Mouton, 1964), pp. 302-7 (see 302).
Midrash Rabbah, ed. H. Freedman and M. Simon (London: Soncino, 1939), pp. 219-20.
J. D. Kingsbury, *The Parables of Jesus in Matthew 13* (Richmond, Virginia: Knox, 1969), p. 4.
R. Jakobson, "The Dominant," *Readings in Russian Poetics: Formalist & Structuralist Views*, ed. L. Matejka and K. Pomorska (Cambridge, Mass.: MIT Press, 1971), p. 87.
155 J. Lyons, *Introduction to Theoretical Linguistics* (London: Cambridge U. Press, 1971), p. 415.
156 W. H. Gass, *Fiction and the Figures of Life* (New York: Knopf, 1970), p. 7.
157 G. T. Hurley, "Buried Treasure Tales in America," *Western Folklore* 10 (1951): 197-216.
T. Rosczak, *Where the Wasteland Ends* (Garden City, N.Y.: Doubleday, 1972), p. 130.
158 E. Wiesel, *The Gates of the Forest* (New York: Avon, 1966).
159 J. E. Irby, *The Structure*, p. 275.
J. L. Borges, in Barrenechea, *Borges the Labyrinth Maker*, p. 151.
160 L. A. Murillo, *The Cyclical Night* (Cambridge, Mass.: Harvard U. Press, 1968), pp. 129-30.
J. E. Irby, *The Structure*, p. 231.
161 J. Jeremias, *The Parables*, p. 138.
162 R. M. Olderman, *Beyond the Waste Land* (New Haven, Conn.: Yale U. Press, 1972), pp. 91-92.
163 R. Christ, *The Narrow Act*, pp. 129-30.
F. Kermode, *The Sense of an Ending* (New York: Oxford U. Press, 1967), p. 88.

Notes

Page
165 J. L. Borges, "Epilogue," *Dt* 93.
E. D. Hirsch, Jr., *Validity in Interpretation* (New Haven, Conn.: Yale U. Press, 1967), pp. 27, 142–44, 210–11, 255.

166 D. Krook, "Intentions and Intentions," *The Theory of the Novel*, pp. 353–72 (see 353).

167 T. S. Eliot, *Tradition and the Individual Talent*, p. 9.
H. James, *The Complete Tales of Henry James*, ed. Leon Edel, vol. 2 (1900–1903) (Philadelphia and New York: Lippincott, 1964), pp. 439–70.
B. Tomashevsky, "Literature and Biography," *Readings in Russian Poetics: Formalist and Structuralist Views*, ed. L. Matejka and K. Pomorska (Cambridge, Mass.: MIT Press, 1971), pp. 47–55 (see 55).
H. Politzer, *Parable and Paradox*, pp. 17–18.

168 E. Dickinson, *The Poems*, vol. 1, p. 327 (#421).
R. Christ, "Borges justified: notes and texts toward stations of a theme," *PFB* 52–87 (see 52–53).

169 C. Wheelock, "Borges' new prose," p. 408.

170 G. Genette, as cited in E. Rodríguez Monegal, "Borges: the reader as writer," *PFB* 102–43 (see 105).

171 D. A. Yates, "Behind 'Borges and I,'" *MFSBN* 317–24.

172 M. S. Staab, *Jorge Luis Borges*, Twayne's World Authors Series 108 (New York: Twayne, 1970), p. 17.
R. Christ, *The Narrow Act*, pp. 57, 84–85.

173 R. Christ, "Borges justified," p. 71.
J. L. Borges, as cited in R. Christ, *The Narrow Act*, p. 11.
R. Howard, "Prose for Borges," *PFB* 9–10.

174 C. Wheelock, *The Mythmaker*, pp. 22, 43, 55, 58, 46 respectively.

175 N. Perrin, *The New Testament: An Introduction* (New York: Harcourt Brace Jovanovich, 1974), p. 278.

178 M. Bakhtin, *Rabelais*, p. 474.

179 E. Dickinson, *The Letters*, vol. 3, p. 847 (#948).
J. Updike, "The Author as Librarian," pp. 236, 238.

Notes

Page

E. Dickinson, *The Poems*, vol. 3, pp. 1065–6 (#1545).

C. Wheelock, *The Mythmaker*, p. 17.

180 W. H. Gass, *Fiction and the Figures*, p. 126.

T. S. Eliot, *Tradition*, p. 9.

Ovid, *Metamorphoses*, trans. F. J. Miller, Loeb Classical Library, 2 vols. (New York: Putnam, 1916), vol. 2 (Books 9–15), pp. 64–125. See Book 10, pp. 40–41, 62–63, 86–90, 143–47; Book 11, pp. 1–59.

181 W. A. Strauss, *Descent and Return: The Orphic Theme in Modern Literature* (Cambridge, Mass.: Harvard U. Press, 1971).

182 I. Hassan, *The Dismemberment of Orpheus: Toward a Postmodern Literature* (New York: Oxford University Press, 1971). See p. 6.

E. Dickinson, *The Poems*, vol. 3, p. 878 (#1261) = *The Letters*, vol. 2, p. 499 (379); *The Poems*, vol. 2, p. 654 (#883); *The Letters*, vol. 2, p. 404 (#261) and p. 436 (#298), respectively, for the four citations.

Abbreviations, Editions, Bibliographies

I. FOR THE STUDY OF JESUS

John	*The Gospel according to John*
Luke	*The Gospel according to Luke*
Mark	*The Gospel according to Mark*
Matt	*The Gospel according to Matthew*
Thom	*The Gospel according to Thomas*

The first four works are canonical gospels and are cited from *The Revised Standard Version of the Bible*. The fifth work is noncanonical and is cited from *The Gospel according to Thomas*. New York: Harper & Row, 1959.

For general bibliography see J. D. Crossan, "A Basic Bibliography for Parables Research," *Semeia* 1 (1974): 236–74.

II. FOR THE STUDY OF BORGES

Aleph	*The Aleph and Other Stories, 1933–1969.* New York: Bantam, 1971.
BIB	*The Book of Imaginary Beings.* New York: Avon, 1969.
DBR	*Doctor Brodie's Report.* New York: Bantam, 1973.
Dt	*Dreamtigers.* New York: Dutton, 1970.
Fic	*Ficciones.* New York: Grove Press, 1962.
Lab	*Labyrinths.* New York: New Directions, 1964.
MFSBN	*Modern Fiction Studies; Jorge Luis Borges Number* 19:3 (Autumn 1973), pp. 313–480.

OI	*Other Inquisitions, 1937–1952.* New York: Simon and Schuster, 1965.
PA	*A Personal Anthology.* New York: Grove Press, 1967.
PFB	*TriQuarterly* 25, (Fall 1972), *Prose for Borges.*
PrDark	*In Praise of Darkness.* New York: Dutton, 1974.

For general bibliographies see Robert L. Fiore, "Toward a Bibliography on Jorge Luis Borges (1923–1969)," *Books Abroad* 45 (1971): 446–66 = *The Cardinal Points of Borges*, Ed. L. Dunham & I. Isaak (Norman, Oklahoma: U. of Oklahoma Press, 1971), pp. 83–105. This is updated by his "Critical Studies on Jorge Luis Borges," *MFSBN* 475–80.

Index of Citations

I. Citations from Jesus

Blessed the Poor (Matt 5:3; Luke 6:20), 74–75
By the Finger of God (Matt 12:28; Luke 11:20), 149
In the Midst of You (Luke 17:20–21; Thom 3; 51; 113), 150–51
On Saving your Life (Mark 8:35; Matt 10:39; 16:25; Luke 9:24; 17:33; John 12:25), 71
The Assassin (Thom 98), 163
The Budding Fig Tree (Mark 13:28; Matt 24:32; Luke 21:29–30), 159
The Evil Tenants (Mark 12:1–12; Matt 21:33–46; Luke 20:9–19; Thom 65), 130, 163
The Eye of the Needle (Mark 10:25; Matt 19:24; Luke 18:25), 70
The Good Samaritan (Luke 10:30–35), 101–4, 106–8
The Great Fish (Matt 13:47–50; Thom 8), 158–59
The Great Supper (Matt 22:1–10; Luke 14:16–24; Thom 64), 111
The Hidden Treasure (Matt 13:44; Thom 109), 153–56
The Kingdom Suffers Violence (Matt 11:12; Luke 16:16), 150–51
The Leaven (Matt 13:33; Luke 13:20–21; Thom 96), 159
The Lost Coin (Luke 15:8–9), 159
The Lost Sheep (Matt 18:12–13; Luke 15:4–6; Thom 107), 159
The Mustard Seed (Mark 4:30–32; Matt 13:31–32; Luke 13:18–19; Thom 20), 159
The Pearl (Matt: 13:45; Thom 76), 158
The Pharisee and the Publican (Luke 18:10–14), 108
The Places at Table (Luke 14:7–11), 111–12
The Prodigal Son (Luke 15:11–32), 110–11
The Rich Man and Lazarus (Luke 16:19–31), 109–110
The Servant Parables (Mark 12:1–8; 13:34–37; Matt 18:23–35; 20:1–13; 21:33–39; 24:45–51; 25:14–30; Luke 12:36–38; 12:42–46; 16:1–7; 17:7–10; 19:12–27; 20:9–15; Thomas 65), 162
The Sower (Mark 4:3–8; Matt 13:3–8; Luke 8:5–8; Thom 9), 128–29, 159

The Vineyard Workers (Matt 20:1–13), 161–62
To Him Who Has (Mark 4:25; Matt 13:12; 25:29; Luke 8:18; 19:26; Thom 41), 70–71
Turning the Other Cheek (Matt 5:39–42; Luke 6:29–30), 65–66, 76

II. Citations from Borges

Afterward (*DBR* 149–52), 78
An Autobiographical Essay (*Aleph* 135–85), v
[A] New Refutation of Time (*OI* 171–87; *Lab* 217–34; *PA* 44–64), 133, 138, 160.
An Examination of the Work of Herbert Quain (*Fic* 73–78), 86, 157
Avatars of the Tortoise (*Lab* 202–8; *OI* 109–115), 30
Averroes' Search (*Lab* 148–55; *PA* 101–110), 23–24, 84
Borges and I [= Borges and Myself] (*Lab* 246–47; *Dt* 51; *Aleph* 98–99 and 201; *PA* 200–201), 171–72
Cambridge (*PrDark* 20–23), 139
Chess (*PA* 75–76; *Dt* 59), 46
Deutsches Requiem (*Lab* 141–47), 80
Doctor Brodie's Report (*DBR* 133–46), 52
Emma Zunz (*Lab* 132–37), 51, 162–63
Epilogue (*Dt* 93), 165
From Allegories to Novels (*OI* 154–57), 117–18
From an Apocryphal Gospel (*PrDark* 106–111), 75–77, 112
Heraclitus (*PrDark* 18–19), 139
Israel (*PrDark* 68–69), 112–13
John 1:14 (*PrDark* 14–17), 170
Jorge Luis Borges (*MFSBN* 317–24), 171
Kafka and His Precursors (*OI* 106–108; *Lab* 199–201), 100
Nathaniel Hawthorne (*OI* 47–65), 100–101, 117
Pedro Salvadores (*Aleph* 122–24 and 205–6; *PrDark* 60–65), 169
Pierre Menard, Author of the *Quixote* (*Fic* 45–55; *Lab* 36–44), 84–85, 141–42
Plain Things (*PrDark* 56–57), 182
Preface (*DBR* ix–xiii), 93, 112, 159
Preface to the 1967 Edition (*BIB* 13–14), 29
Prologue (*Fic* 15–16), 88

The Aleph (*Aleph* 3–17 and 188–90; *PA* 138–54), 45
The Analytical Language of John Wilkins (*OI* 101–5), 9
The Approach to Al-Mu'tasim (*Fic* 37–43); *Aleph* 27–33 and 192), 81–83, 84, 85, 173
The Circular Ruins (*Lab* 45–50; *PA* 68–74; *Fic* 57–63), 51, 53, 87
The Duel (*DBR* 31–40), 151–52
The End (*Fic* 159–62; *PA* 166–69), 169
The End of the Duel (*DBR* 43–50), 162
The Fearful Sphere of Pascal (*Lab* 189–92; *OI* 6–9), 27, 116
The First Wells (*OI* 86–88), 101
The Garden of the Forking Paths (*Fic* 89–101; *Lab* 19–29), 80–81, 86, 133, 139, 156–57
The Gospel according to Mark (*DBR* 3–13), 100
The Immortal (*Lab* 105–18), 152–53
The Immortals (*Aleph* 109–14 and 203–4), 152
The Intruder (*Aleph* 103–8 and 202–3; *DBR* 67–74), 162
The Library of Babel (*Fic* 79–88; *Lab* 51–58), 90–91, 141
The Maker (*Aleph* 100–2 and 202), 88
The Man on the Threshold (*Aleph* 85–90 and 199–200), 139–40, 142
Theme of the Traitor and the Hero (*Fic* 123–27; *Lab* 72–75), 83–84
The Other Death (*Aleph* 67–74 and 197–98), 160–61
The Sect of the Phoenix (*Fic* 163–66; *Lab* 101–4), 9–11
The Wall and the Books (*OI* 3–5; *Lab* 186–88; *PA* 89–92), 169
Three Versions of Judas (*Fic* 151–57; *Lab* 95–100), 87–88, 146
Tlön, Uqbar, Orbius Tertius (*Lab* 3–18; *Fic* 17–35), 52–53, 79–80, 171
To Israel (*PrDark* 66–67), 113

Index of Authors

Abrams, M. 122
Alazraki, J. 142
Ammons, A. R. 5
Anderson, R. 151
Aristotle 12, 14, 15, 21, 68, 153
Auden, W. H. 19
Augustine 133, 144
Ayora, J. R. 50, 141

Bakhtin, M. 19, 37, 126, 178
Barrenechea, A. M. 118, 140, 142
Barth, J. 3
Barthes, R. 3, 39–40, 102, 127
Beagle, P. S. xiii, 125, 138, 153
Beardslee, W. A. 72
Beardsley, M. C. 91
Beaufret, J. 68
Beckett, S. 32
Belitt, B. 114
Benveniste, E. 39
Bergson, H. 14
Bloom, H. 61
Brecht, B. 131
Burgin, R. 88

Cameron, A. 12
Camus, A. 68, 94–95, 107
Cavell, S. 32
Chesterton, G. K. 117–119
Christ, R. 50, 88, 118, 141, 163, 168, 172–73

Cioran, E. M. 4
Coover, R. 123
Cornford, F. M. 21
Crespy, G. 34
Croce, B. 117

de Man, P. 117
Derrida, J. 34
de Saussure, F. 38
Dickinson, E. 77, 94, 148, 150, 168, 179
di Giovanni, N. T. 138
D'Lugo, M. 83
Dohmann, B. 50, 78

Ehrmann, J. 26
Eissfeldt, O. 58
Eliot, T. S. ii, 42, 61, 167, 180
Erlich, V. 41

Fielding, H. 105–6
Fink, E. 27–28
Fiore, R. L. 184
Fletcher, A. 119–20
Fowler, A. 62
Frost, R. 92, 148
Fry, C. 17
Frye, N. 18
Funk, R. W. xiii
Gass, W. H. 156, 180
Genette, G. 170
Greimas, A. J. xv

205

Guillén, C. 62
Güttgemanns, E. XIV

Halliday, M. A. K. 154
Harss, L. 50, 78
Hassan, I. 182
Hawthorne, N. 100–1, 107, 116–18
Heidegger, M. 68–69
Heraclitus 28, 68
Hinman, L. M. 142–43
Hirsch, E. D. 165
Honig, E. 121
Howard, R. 173
Huizinga, J. 25–26, 28
Hurley, G. T. 157
Huxley, A. 21
Hyers, C. 46

Irby, J. 51, 114, 159–60
Isaacs, N. D. 144

Jakobson, R. 107–8, 154
James, H. 122, 167
Jameson, F. XIV
Jeremias, J. 109, 161
Jolles, A. 69

Kafka, F. 3, 88, 95, 100–1, 107, 112, 114, 123–25, 127
Kellogg, R. 116
Kermode, F. 163
Kierkegaard, S. 47
Kingsbury, J. D. 154
Koestler, A. 18
Krieger, M. 61
Krook, D. 166
Kuhn, T. S. XIV

Lanham, R. A. 43
Leach, E. 98
Lévi-Strauss, C. 34, 98
Lewald, H. E. 144
Lima, R. 118
Lyon, T. E. 78
Lyons, J. 155

Maranda, P. 98
Marrois, A. 88
Martin, R. 11, 16
Miles, Jr., J. 96
Murillo, L. A. 144, 160
Murrin, M. 120–1

Natella, Jr., A. A. 151
Nietzsche, F. 93, 142–44

Oderman, R. E. 162
Olrik, A. 65
Otto, R. 43

Perrin, N. 149, 175
Peterkiewicz, J. 4, 50
Piaget, J. 33
Plato 11–12, 16, 28
Plessner, H. 136, 149
Politzer, H. 93–97, 101, 113, 123–24, 127, 167
Poulet, G. 3
Pound, E. 73
Puech, H.-C. 135

Quispel, G. 145

Rabkin, E. S. 13
Reid, A. 79

Ricoeur, P.   xv, 102
Rilke, R. M.   50, 92, 98, 151
Robbe-Grillet, A.   18
Rodríquez-Monegal, E.   50
Roszak, T.   157

Scholes, R.   39, 69, 84, 116
Scott, Jr., N. A.   21
Shklovsky, V.   40–51, 63, 126
Sontag, S.   4, 49
Sophocles   12–15
Sosnowski, S.   89
Stabb, M. S.   172
Stark, J.   81
Sternberg, M.   41
Stevens, W.   81
Strauss, W. A.   181
Swabey, M. C.   33
Sypher, W.   17–19, 21, 31, 33, 75

Todorov, T.   42, 61, 91, 102–3
Tolstoy, L.   104
Tomashevsky, B.   41, 167
Turner, D. E.   45, 91
Turner, V. W.   35, 39, 99

Updike, J.   91, 179

van der Leeuw, G.   135, 137
Vernant, J.-P.   15
Via, Jr., D. O.   xiii
Vonnegut, K.   14, 20, 35, 45–46

Weber, F. W.   53–54, 89
Wells, H. G.   101
Welsford, E.   11
Wheelock, C.   51, 119, 169, 174, 179–80
Wiesel, E.   158
Wilde, O.   20
Wilder, A.   xiii
Wimsatt, W. K.   91

Yates, D. A.   171
Yeats, W. B.   30, 73, 99

www.ingramcontent.com/pod-product-compliance
Lightning Source LLC
Chambersburg PA
CBHW070315230426
43663CB00011B/2142